The ABCs of Montessori and Special Needs

By: Renae M Eddy

Every Star Is Different
http://everystarisdifferent.com
everystarisdifferent4@gmail.com

Disclaimer: Any advice or suggestions that we write here CANNOT be considered therapy or professional consultation, due to counseling ethics standards. What we hope to
offer is our personal experience as parents of children with PTSD, combined with tips
from Jason's education, professional background and experience. Consult with your
child's doctor or mental health therapist before attempting to diagnose or provide treatment to your child.

The ABCs of Montessori and Special Needs

Introduction

    Thank You

    My Panel of Certified Montessori Teachers

    Our Story

Special Needs in the Classroom

The ABCs

    Auditory Stimuli

    Behaviors

    Chronological and Cognitive Age

    Developmental Age

    Emotional Age

    Fine Motor Skills

    Gross Motor Skills

    Home Environment

    Incentives and Reinforcers

    Juggling Multiple Special Needs

    Kid Safety

    Lessons

    Materials and Manipulatives

    Nonfiction

    Olfactory and Oral Stimuli

Proprioceptive Stimuli

Questions

Rotation of Materials and Activities

Stimming and Self-Regulation

Tactile Stimuli

Unit Studies

Vestibular and Visual Stimuli

Writing

Extra Tidbits

Yes!

Zero Exceptions

Thank You

This book would not be a reality if it weren't for the help and support of my husband, Jason Eddy. I could not have written this without him. Jason wrote the Special Needs in the Classroom section of this book and also contributed input and feedback during the writing and editing processes. He is my partner in all things including the implementation of Montessori in our home and classroom.

Jason has a master's degree in Marriage and Family Counseling and is a Licensed Mental Health Counselor in NY. He has spent 10 years working as a therapist to adults and children, in a private and group counseling sessions, and in residential facilities. Currently Jason works with me homeschooling our four children with special needs and writes for the website www.everystarisdifferent.com.

My Panel of Certified Montessori Teachers

I am not a certified Montessori instructor. My experience with Montessori comes from six years of homeschooling my children paired with constant study and research. One of my biggest concerns while writing this book was making sure that my thoughts, opinions, and recommendations were in line with Montessori principles. The professionals listed below volunteered their time and expertise answering my questions about specific aspects of the Montessori Method. It is with their help that I feel confident stating that ideas in this book are faithful to the spirit of Maria Montessori's work, and consistent with the training of certified Montessori teachers.

Members of the panel have not read this book prior to publishing. In no way have they stated that they endorse what I have written.

Shawn Hummel enjoys living in rural Ohio with her husband and daughter. In the summer they can often be found outside gardening or doing other things together on their farm bordered property. They also enjoy eating, sharing and processing the fresh vegetables during the warm months. Colder times are frequently spent doing home improvements or reading from their extensive library of used books.

Shawn has AMI Montessori training for ages 3-6 and 6-12 as well as teaching experience at various levels. Shawn attended a Montessori school from ages 2 ½ - 6 and considers that an important foundation for her life. Her passion for Montessori becomes clear when asked about anything relating to the topic; she will tell you as much as you want to know. In recent years Shawn has moved away from teaching full time so that she can raise her daughter and run her business.

Montessori Materials by Request is an Etsy shop full of items that Shawn has developed and makes with her own hands. There you will find cloth pouches for displaying materials as well as some of the early language materials themselves (in both finished and PDF forms). Maria Montessori was a big believer in attracting the children to the work which often means offering something that is different, nicer and more colorful than they might find in their daily lives. Shawn completely agrees with this and offers beautiful pouches in many colors that work well with Montessori items. You can find her work at https://www.etsy.com/shop/montessorimaterial.

Maria Burke, M. Ed., is an AMS 3-12 certified teacher. She also has Bachelor's degrees in Elementary Education and French as well as a Master's in Curriculum Education. She teaches Upper Elementary in Nashville, TN. She is also the Director of Lighthouse Learning, LLC, a company that specializes in supplemental educational and proprioceptive materials including The Dollar Board (TM), a complete curriculum to teach children to count money, concretely and independently, as well as Grammar Proficiency, a leveled grammar program based on the Primary Phonics books. You can find her work at www.lighthouselearningllc.com, on Facebook at https://www.facebook.com/lighthouselearningllc/ and on Instagram @lighthouselearningllc.

Lisa Dei Gratia is a Montessori and state trained teacher who lives in New Zealand. Lisa has a passion for making Montessori accessible for all people and for incorporating indigenous perspectives in the classroom. Her main experience is in Public School Montessori Elementary Teaching. Lisa is the owner of Montessorikiwi.com and sells resources for Preschool and Elementary at https://www.teacherspayteachers.com/Store/Montessorikiwi.

Michelle Rugel-Hiatt received her M.Ed. from Loyola University and was trained as an AMI elementary guide by Dr. Kay Baker at the Washington Montessori Institute. She taught in an elementary classroom in Chicago and helped to organize a new Montessori environment in Switzerland before moving to Puebla, Mexico for her AMI primary training under Coral Ruiz. She has since been a primary guide at the Montessori Academy Bangkok International School in Thailand and is currently enrolled in the Assistants to Infancy program with Judi Orion in Denver, CO during the summer months.

In an effort to bring beautiful Montessori materials into the homes and classrooms of Montessorians around the world Michelle created The Montessori Company. TMC was established to make it easier for guides and parents to fill their environments with truly exceptional materials, from hand-drawn illustrations to books and other Montessori products. Michelle and her team are dedicated to creating the most beautiful, thoughtful and philosophically consistent materials, and making them easily accessible so that the "convenient" materials can also be the best materials. You can view work at https://www.themontessoricompany.com.

Ashley Speed is an AMI-trained 3-6 guide, who is currently at home with her first baby. After struggling to find card materials she loved for use in her own classroom, she started Diamond Montessori- a company dedicated to making inclusive, diverse and beautiful language, cultural and scientific materials. Follow her on Instagram- @diamondmontessori or check out her store on Etsy-www.etsy.com/ca/shop/diamondmontessori.

Matt Bronsil is a 3-6 Montessori teacher in Taiwan. He runs a Montessori blog at www.MontessoriMatt.com and teachers online courses for parents and teachers at www.MontessoriWebinars.com.

Our Story

If someone told me 15 years ago, how my life would be today, I'm not quite sure how I would have responded. Perhaps run the other way? Cry? Be angry? Or just maybe I would have said okay, and spent as much time as possible studying and learning all I could, in hopes that it would prepare me for what I do now, 24 hours a day, seven days a week.

But then I wonder. If I had known, would I be able to find the joy in the journey? Would I consider my children to be the blessings they are? It's then that I feel at peace knowing all has worked out the way it was intended.

I am a happily married, work-at-home mom, who homeschools my four children with special needs. My first two children, Dinomite, age nine, and Bulldozer, age eight, are biological children. Both were diagnosed with autism, Dinomite at age three and Bulldozer at age two.

The boys also have ADHD. Dinomite has an anxiety disorder. Bulldozer has a lack of safety awareness, lack of motor planning, and auditory processing issues. Dinomite and Bulldozer have very different obsessions, sensory issues, and autism symptoms. Someone once exclaimed,

"Once you've met one child with autism, you've met one child with autism."

That proves to be very true with Dinomite and Bulldozer. Dinomite is my animal lover. For the longest time it was dinosaurs, then he started studying all the other prehistoric creatures and sea monsters. Eventually he moved on to amphibians and reptiles. Now he's branched out to birds and so many other species.

When he was little, his other obsession was vehicles, preferably emergency vehicles. This obsession led to the introduction of LEGO, from which there appears to be no end. *Star Wars*, *Harry Potter*, *Lord of the Rings*, *The Hobbit* and superheroes of any kind also entertain Dinomite.

Dinomite has a few food allergies, but nothing that I worry about on a regular basis. Food allergies don't compare to other struggles he has with food due to sensory issues. I've never known a child so content with eating the same thing day in and day out. Some type of food therapy will most likely be in his future.

Bulldozer loves weather and astronomy. He has very visual obsessions, including water, waves, and whales. His little kid obsession was vehicles, preferably construction vehicles. He also loves all things LEGO *Star Wars*, *Harry Potter*, *Lord of the Rings* and *The Hobbit*.

Bulldozer was born with over 35 allergies to foods, some very severe and life threatening. At 18 months it was discovered that he has a life threatening allergy to adhesives (band aids, stickers, tape, glue, etc.)

As Bulldozer has grown older, he has grown out of some allergies including dairy, eggs, nuts, and tree nuts, while other allergies have become more severe. Some new food allergies have also been added to the list.

Bulldozer has severe environmental allergies that inhibit his ability to function during the spring, summer, and fall. We call him our "Bubble Boy."

When Bulldozer was about six months old, I felt the impression that another child was waiting to come to our family, a baby girl. I had been advised not to have more children, due to my own health issues. My husband and I decided to look into adoption. (This was before the boys' autism was diagnosed.)

After researching all of our options, we decided to adopt through the foster care system. This decision changed our lives. We became foster parents for four years, caring for over 20 children. More than half were infants. Two of these infants are now our adopted daughters, Princess, age seven, and Sunshine, age four.

Princess came to us at six months. She was a very difficult baby. Most of her needs were not medically based. It didn't take long before we recognized that something wasn't quite right.

One month after learning of the boys' diagnoses of autism, we learned that Princess has Reactive Attachment Disorder (RAD) and Post Traumatic Stress Disorder (PTSD). Over time, she also developed an anxiety disorder.

I will always remember the developmental pediatrician looking at me wide eyed, as she learned the adoption wasn't 100% complete on diagnosis day.

"Are you SURE you want to do this? This will be the hardest thing you've ever had to do."

With tears in my eyes, I said I was sure. There has never been any doubt in my mind that Princess was meant to be our daughter.

The developmental pediatrician was right. Raising a child with RAD, PTSD, and an anxiety disorder has been one of the hardest things I have ever done, or probably ever will do. I am the target of Princess' rage and frustration.

There are moments that make it all worth it. When we have them, I'm sure to capture the moments with photos. Princess is brilliant. She is beautiful. Her imagination is endless. Princess' interests are never limited to just a few. She LOVES to read anything she can get her hands on.

Sunshine was the last infant to enter our home. She came at six months of age also. Though separated from her parents at birth, Sunshine endured other hardships in a foster home previous to ours. Her adoption process was very quick.

Sunshine was born with a very mild case of Cranial Facial Microsomia and suffers from a vision impairment in her right eye. As preparations for her adoption moved forward she appeared to be doing extremely well, with only small delays. However, shortly after the adoption, it became very apparent that something was wrong.

Sunshine was tested for food allergies at two and a half years old. She tested positive for fourteen foods/groups Many are different than Bulldozer's food allergies.

At the age of 29 months, Sunshine was diagnosed with Autism Spectrum Disorder (ASD), Reactive Attachment Disorder (RAD), Post Traumatic Stress Disorder (PTSD), and a sleep disorder. She was given an official mood disorder diagnosis at age four.

Sunshine is the most delayed of my children. Unlike her siblings, she is physically aggressive and rages often. A significant amount of time and energy is spent training and implementing strategies that will help Sunshine thrive, while keeping everyone safe. My husband is now home full time to help with this. He is Sunshine's main target.

When Sunshine is doing well, she's in love with babies, cats and dogs. She is also obsessed with Stitch from *Lilo and Stitch.* Sunshine always has to have a paper in her hands, whether a receipt from the store or a book.

We've closed the doors of our home to foster children knowing our four will take all the energy and effort my husband and I have, to raise and teach full time. Our lives are dedicated to teaching our children, not only academics but life skills using the Montessori Method. We hope one day they can all be independent and successful on their own.

Special Needs in the Classroom

Special needs is a term that covers the broad variety of medical, developmental, psychological, emotional and social problems that limit a child's ability to function appropriately in an educational setting.

All students have ups and downs over the course of their academic career. Everyone has bad days. What distinguishes these sorts of problems from the issues experienced by a child with special needs is the severity and duration. Many of the special needs listed below have lifelong implications, and affect individuals in all areas of life, not just in the classroom.

Neurodevelopmental Disorders

Neurodevelopmental Disorder is a relatively new term in the world of special needs. It was introduced in 2013 in the Diagnostic and Statistical Manual, Fifth Revision (also known as DSM-V), published by the American Psychiatric Association. Major advances in the understanding of brain development and functioning over the past 10-15 years led the authors of the DSM-V to introduce the term, to describe a host of conditions and disorders that have problems in brain development in early childhood as their common cause.

This emphasis on neurological functioning has dramatically changed the way that many psychological disorders are viewed and treated today. The following is a brief review of the major categories of neurodevelopmental disorders that teachers in all settings will encounter in their classrooms at some time or another. They all have serious implications for a child's educational aptitude and overall ability to function in school.

Intellectual Disabilities

Intellectual disability (ID) is the term used to describe limitations that a person has in thinking, communication, social interactions, self-care and adaptive skills. The causes are varied. Some are genetic. Others are due to problems during pregnancy, childbirth, and early infancy. Intellectual disabilities can also be the result of an early childhood illness. Whatever the reason, a child with ID develops physically and cognitively more slowly than his peers.

In previous editions of the DSM, various types of problems with cognitive skills were listed separately from one another. One could be diagnosed with mental retardation, development delay, specific learning disability, etc. each seeming to exist in its own little world, separate and independent of any other disorder. The authors of DSM-V have shifted away from that kind of thinking.

Now all issues with intellectual disability in early childhood are considered neurodevelopmental problems. The differences are in specific types of functioning and severity. A child who struggles specifically with writing could meet criteria for an intellectual disability in writing. A child that in previous years would be diagnosed with mental retardation is now considered to have a severe intellectual disability.

Communication Disorders

There are four kinds of communication disorders identified in DSM-V:

1. **Language disorder**– There are two subtypes in this category: expressive language disorder and receptive language disorder. Problems with producing verbal language is called expressive language disorder. Problems with understanding verbal language is receptive language disorder.

2. **Social communication disorder** is concerned with pragmatics and social conventions associated with verbal communication. Formerly considered a trait of Asperger's syndrome and other related disorders, it is now classified as a stand-alone communication disorder.

3. **Speech-sound disorder** is a diagnosis that involves problems with making the appropriate sounds in verbal language which continues beyond age five. A child with this disorder is hard to understand when he is speaking.

4. **Stuttering** is pretty self-explanatory. It covers problems with pauses in the middle of words, hesitance at the beginning of words, as well as repetition of whole words or phrases. It also includes involuntary facial tension or tics that occur when the child is speaking.

Attention Deficit Hyperactivity Disorder

Attention deficit hyperactivity disorder (ADHD) is one of the most common psychiatric disorders among children. It has undergone numerous changes over the years, as our understanding of the underlying causes and mechanism of the disorder have improved. For DSM-V, ADHD was included as a type of Neurodevelopmental Disorder. The language here is meaningful, as the focus of treatment has changed from hyperactivity to addressing problems in higher order thinking or executive functioning, which is the central trait of ADHD. In the classroom, impulsivity, distractedness and disorganized planning and thinking are the major obstacles to learning posed by ADHD.

Motor Disorder

The motor or tic disorders have been placed under the neurodevelopmental umbrella as well. The terms for these disorders remain intact from previous editions of DSM. The motor disorders are notable for teachers insofar as they impede a child's ability to perform fine motor tasks such as writing due to safety risks to the child. There is a possibility of injury due to a sudden tic or motor movement, such as head banging. Motor disorders are not typically associated with learning disabilities or other intellectual disabilities in general. However they frequently co-occur with other disabilities or disorders that do involve academic problems. The motor disorders are:

1. **Developmental coordination disorder** is marked by delays or major difficulty with gross motor and fine motor skills. Other symptoms include general clumsiness when walking, running, crawling, etc.

2. **Stereotypic movement disorder** includes symptoms such as head banging, rocking back and forth, nail biting, hair biting, and other kinds of hitting or shaking oneself. In the classroom, the primary concern is safety for the child and others nearby. Educational problems are not necessarily part of stereotypic movement disorder. Care should be taken to distinguish these behaviors from stimming or self-regulatory behaviors.

3. **Tourette syndrome** involves a number of simple and complex motor and vocal tics. The concern for teachers is the complex tics, which can sometimes be quite sudden and intense, involving head and shoulder movement, bending twisting, hopping etc. Considera-

tions should be made to ensure the child's safety in the learning environment.

4. **Persistent vocal or motor tic disorder** is a label used when the tics seen in Tourette syndrome and other tic disorders are either vocal or motor, not both. Precautions are to be taken with regards to the complex motor tics.

5. **Provisional tic disorder** (formerly transient tic disorder) is another version of motor or verbal tic disorder, but the tics do not occur chronically or persistently.

Global Developmental Delay

Global developmental delay (GDD) is a term used specifically with children under age five. GDD is diagnosed when there are notable delays in motor, intellectual, social and emotional functioning skills. GDD is usually diagnosed by pediatricians and other related specialties, and commonly results in a referral to the local agency responsible for early intervention services. Specialists in occupational therapy, physical therapy, and others are then brought into the child's home, conducting assessments, developing treatment plans and providing the recommended services. It is important to find out if the child is receiving early intervention services at home, in order to understand where there are specific areas of weakness and to collaborate with other specialists on the team.

Autism Spectrum Disorder

Autism Spectrum Disorder (ASD) has emerged in the DSM-V to replace outdated terms such as Asperger's syndrome, pervasive developmental disorder, and high-functioning autism. ASD is yet another blanket term that covers symptoms and traits that used to be unique diagnoses, but are now recognized as a broad array of impairments of neurological development in early childhood. A child with ASD might have any combination of motor tics, intellectual deficits and communication problems common to the disorders that are listed above. A few key traits are unique to some children who have ASD, including:

- Sensory processing issues
- Special dietary needs
- Strict adherence to specific rituals and routines

- Self-soothing or self-regulatory behaviors (not considered involuntary like tics)

Some children with ASD do not have an intellectual disability. ASD is diagnosed when there are significant deficits in two or more neurological domains, but not necessarily intellectual functioning. There are some individuals with ASD that have an IQ in the genius range of 130 or above, yet struggle severely in other areas.

Anxiety-Based Disorders

Anxiety based disorders that interfere with a child's ability to function in the classroom include panic disorder, generalized anxiety disorder (GAD), social phobia, and specific phobia. Obsessive-compulsive disorder is an anxiety disorder with fewer implications for school functioning, except where the compulsive behaviors take so much of the child's time and energy that he is unable to focus and work on assignments. As a rule, all other areas of functioning are in the normal range when it comes to academics and behavioral expectations at school. Unless the child has school phobia, in which case, your biggest hurdle is probably truancy.

1. **Panic disorder** is diagnosed when someone has panic attacks. This is described as a period of intense fear along with other physiological and/or psychological changes that occur within ten minutes of the onset of the panic attack. Incidence of panic attacks can range widely; from a few per year to several every day. To meet full criteria, the attacks have to be accompanied by one or both of the following traits. One, the person consistently thinks about the consequences of the panic attack and worries about having another one. Two, the person's behavior changes dramatically, in efforts to avoid having another panic attack. The behaviors severely impact the person's ability to function at work, at school, etc.

2. Specific phobia is a condition that is diagnosed when a person has an irrational fear of a particular thing or situation, felt so intensely that the person gets anxious or has a panic attack just thinking about it. In DSM-V, it is not necessary that the person understands that the fear is irrational in order to meet criteria for the diagnosis. This is an important change from previous editions of DSM, and a major benefit

when it comes to children, who sometimes have a hard time discerning between reality and fiction, rational and irrational.

3. Social phobia is a disorder characterized by intense fear and anxiety about social situations and performance in social settings. The person is worried about being humiliated or embarrassed in front of other people, to the extent that he goes out of his way to avoid the situation, and endures it with great anxiety when it is unavoidable. The phobia can cause anxiety or panic attacks, and great lengths are taken by the person to avoid the feared situations, leading to problems at school, work, etc.

4. Generalized anxiety disorder (GAD) is the term used to describe a steady feeling or worry and fear that persists more days than not for at least six months. The disorder involves symptoms that go beyond just feeling nervous. To meet the full criteria, physiological symptoms including sleeplessness, gastrointestinal discomfort, feeling weary or fatigued all the time, etc. have to be present, along with difficulty concentrating and feeling "stuck." The six month duration is key here, as most people have bouts with anxiety and worry from time to time, but these usually last far less six months.

Trauma and Stressor-related Disorders

One of the major features of DSM-V was the introduction of a new category of disorders, headlined by post-traumatic stress disorder (PTSD). Grouping trauma and stress disorders together reflects the major advancements that have been achieved in understanding how the brain reacts to stress and traumatic events.

Post Traumatic Stress Disorder

A phenomenon associated mostly with veterans of combat, Post Traumatic Stress Disorder (PTSD) is understood much differently now than it was about 100 years ago, when it was known as shell shock or battle fatigue. Children who experience traumatic events, or witness a single life-threatening or traumatizing event, are as prone to developing PTSD as the most hardened combat veterans.

For the first time, a pre-school subtype of PTSD has been identified in DSM-V. The symptoms are dramatically different than adult PTSD. Regardless of when the PTSD problem began, this diagnosis comes with painful consequences for the child and his entire family. Of concern to teachers is the unpredictable and potentially explosive possibility of a traumatic flashback in the classroom. PTSD is diagnosed when traumatic symptoms are seen at least six months after the traumatizing event first occurred.

Acute Stress Disorder

Acute stress disorder describes many of the same symptoms of PTSD, except that they begin shortly after the traumatic event happens. Being aware of potentially traumatizing events that have occurred with a child and family is key to understanding what one might expect in terms of behaviors, and the best ways to intervene and provide help.

Adjustment Disorders

An adjustment disorder is a term used to describe an adverse reaction to some event or situation that is either new or ongoing. There are four identified types of adjustment disorder.

1. **Adjustment disorder** with depressed mood is diagnosed when the child has been showing sad or listless moods and major changes in activity level and participation in desired activities over a period of time. The cause could be anything that the child finds difficult to understand or cope with effectively.

2. **Adjustment disorder with anxiety** is similar to the previous disorder, except with anxiety rather than depressed mood.

3. **Adjustment disorder with disturbance of conduct** is different in that the child acts out behaviorally rather than internalizing the frustration as depressed moods or anxiety. This form of adjustment disorder is expected with younger children. They are just developing emotional regulation and communication skills and find those difficult enough without having to cope with whatever is causing the disturbance.

4. **Adjustment disorder with mixed features** is a category used for any traits of mood or anxiety symptoms listed above, combined with conduct problems.

The key trait of an adjustment disorder is that whatever circumstances are fueling the mood or conduct disturbance do not have to be traumatic. It only has to be just overwhelming enough that the child can't function in other areas of life while it's ongoing.

An adjustment disorder is not a sign of an underlying psychiatric condition. It is more like the brain telling the child that something very uncomfortable is happening and he needs to do something about it. In other words, an adjustment disorder is a call for help from a body that lacks a coping strategy or way out of a tough situation. Communication with the family is key if you notice new or unexplainable behaviors in a child. Symptoms of an adjustment disorder disappear with time as the child develops new coping strategies and supports.

Reactive Attachment Disorder

Reactive Attachment Disorder (RAD) combines aspects of early childhood trauma, brain damage and PTSD rolled into one. It has been divided into two subtypes, depending on cause of the disorder and how the child relates to strangers and new adults.

1. **Reactive attachment disorder (RAD)** is when a child struggles to find trust in people in general, and in parents and other authority figures in particular. If parental care is abusive, or inconsistent, the child is left with his needs unfulfilled. As the pattern continues, he realizes quickly that asking for help to meet those needs is futile, if not outright dangerous. The fundamental trust that is normally established in the child's first few weeks of life has been undone, forever affecting the child's relationship with himself and everyone around him. The neural pathways that are developing in the infant's mind have been fundamentally altered just as they are being formed, resulting in permanent damage throughout the brain. A child with RAD seeks to dominate and maintain control over every relationship he has, especially when it comes to adult authority figures, such as parents or teachers.

2. **Disinhibited social engagement disorder** is a new description in DSM-V that is an offshoot of the old RAD diagnostic criteria. The cause of the behaviors in this case is neglect (not abuse) in infancy and early childhood. This can occur when the care of the child changes hands frequently, as in the case of orphans and children in foster care. The first and most distinctive feature of this disorder is intense shyness around new adults. As time wears on, the shyness is

replaced with reluctance to join with adults in any way that is emotionally close or sensitive. Other behaviors associated with RAD are
also seen with this disorder.

Mood Disorders and Emotional Disturbances

Mood disorders include depressive disorder, bipolar I disorder,
bipolar II disorder, cyclothymic disorder, and mood disorder with mixed
features. These are diagnosed mostly in adults, although child diagnosis
of bipolar disorder is becoming more common. Mood disorders are characterized by an inability to maintain emotions, as well as difficulty with
energy level, motivation, and overall level of functioning. Below is a list
of the mood disorders listed in DSM-V.

1. **Major depressive disorder** is a persistent sad anxious mood with
   or without suicidal thoughts, that lasts for at least two weeks. In children, an irritable or anxious mood can be seen rather than a sad
   mood.

2. **Dysthymia** (persistent depressive disorder) is a low level depressed mood that has less impact on daily functioning than major
   depression, but persists for much longer.

3. **Premenstrual dysphoric disorder** is a new term for symptoms of
   depression that coincide with a woman's menstrual cycle. Clearly
   this is not something considered with young children.

4. **Depressive disorder due to another medical condition** is seen
   when a medical condition is the only antecedent to the onset of depressive symptoms.

5. **Substance/Medication-induced depressive disorder** occurs when
   depressive traits are seen as a side effect of medication. Medication
   changes can be communicated between parents and teacher to keep
   school personnel attentive to any signs of these side effects in the
   child.

6. **Unspecified depressive disorder** is a set of symptoms that meet
   some but not all of the criteria of any of the disorders listed above.

   The bipolar disorders in DSM-V are as follows.

1. **Bipolar I disorder** is diagnosed when an individual has one full-
   blown manic episode at any time in life, followed by at least one in-

stance of depressed moods that persist for more than two weeks. There are different subtypes and feature specifiers, but the heart of the diagnosis is the presence of the full manic and full depressed episodes.

2. **Bipolar II disorder** is diagnosed when a hypomanic episode (manic moods, but not quite as intense or long-lived as a full manic episode) is followed by a depressed or dysthymic mood that persists for two weeks or more. Bipolar II is more common and diagnosed more frequently.

3. **Mood disorder not otherwise specified (NOS)** is a term used when full criteria for bipolar I or II are not fully met, but most of the traits are there, especially the cycling between depressed and near-manic moods.

4. **Disruptive mood regulation disorder** is a new diagnosis introduced in DSM-V, for use with children from ages 6-18, where most, but not all, of the criteria for bipolar disorder are met. The symptoms are more inline with the things that are seen most often with children than the criteria for adults.

Emotional disturbance is another term that is heard frequently in education settings. It is used specifically in U.S. Special Education law, and includes the mood disorders and some anxiety-based disorders. The difference in terms is important, since in the U.S., emotional disturbance is the key to opening up resources and materials via special education services.

It may seem strange to talk about mood disorders in young children. After all, many of the mood disorders aren't manifest in people until they reach their early 20s. It's also true that some emotional regulation problems in early childhood resolve themselves as a child matures and brain functioning improves. Most of the time though, signs of a mood disorder in young children evolve into a full-blown mood disorder in adolescence and adulthood. Let it be known that a young child can be diagnosed with a mood disorder.

The mood disorders are especially challenging for early childhood education professionals for two reasons. One, the intensity and frequency of behaviors and verbal output with these disorders is quite high and becomes wearying over time. Two, depression and mania in early childhood can look quite different than it does in later years. Unlike adolescents and adults, young children with bipolar disorder are always manic, rarely sleeping, constantly in motion, chattering incessantly, and inconsistent and unpredictable in temperament and actions. Children with depression often appear agitated or angry, rather than sad or fatigued.

Physical Impairments

This category covers several areas that are considered individually in the special education world, but are gathered together here for convenience. There is a huge variety of medical conditions and physical impairments that adversely affect a child's ability to learn. Some are present from birth, others acquired through illness or disease, and some that result from accident or injury.

1. **Visual impairment** is defined as low or poor vision that cannot be corrected to normal vision with glasses or any other corrective lenses.

2. **Blindness** is used to describe a range of vision problems, from total sightlessness up to a maximum of one-tenth of normal eye function with corrective lenses. It is also defined simply as the lack of useful eye function.

3. **Auditory impairment** is defined as any hearing loss below 90 decibels. Auditory impairment can be permanent, transient, conditional, or fluctuating

4. **Deafness** is defined in special education law as hearing loss above 90 decibels.

5. **Deaf-blindness** is defined as loss of hearing above 90 decibels and vision that cannot be corrected to normal level with corrective lenses.

6. **Orthopedic impairment** is any issue related to development or functional problems in the skeletal or muscular systems, including congenital problems (like spina bifida), problems caused by disease or other medical causes (such as cerebral palsy), etc.

7. **Other health impairment** is the term used for problems in school functioning and attendance due to the nature of certain medical conditions such as leukemia, epilepsy, heart conditions, etc.

8. **Traumatic Brain Injury**– This refers to problems with cognitive, emotional and social functioning due to damage sustained in an accident or injury.

Each of these conditions has unique implications for classroom functioning and learning. The solutions and resources are just as varied and unique as the causes. In the vast majority of cases, these conditions are known and have been addressed in some form long before the child enters the classroom, and specific procedures should be determined case by case.

Auditory Stimuli

Auditory refers to the sense of hearing. Stimulus is something in the environment that provokes a reaction from an organ or tissue in the body. Auditory stimuli are sounds in an environment that affect an individual.

A child with special needs may struggle with auditory stimuli in the classroom. He may be extremely sensitive to noise in general or may have strong reactions to specific sounds, avoiding them at all costs. Another child may crave auditory stimuli. In this case the child will do all he can to receive the auditory stimuli his body needs.

It is possible that a child with special needs struggles with an auditory processing disorder. The term auditory processing refers to how the body recognizes and interprets sounds in the environment. A child who suffers from an auditory processing disorder has difficulties understanding what is said by others. Difficulties are made even more complicated in situations where there are multiple layers of auditory stimuli. A child with auditory processing disorder may not be able to filter out various sounds in the environment. This results in the inability to respond accurately and in a timely manner during conversations.

Auditory Stimuli in the Montessori Classroom

A Montessori classroom is buzzing with activity, but the noise level is generally low. If the students are engaged and working, they are focused, concentrating and quiet.

Lessons are presented in small groups or individually. This helps with issues related to focus, distractibility and auditory processing disorder. The volume level of the classroom stays low as the teacher does not need to raise her voice to reach every student. The focus of lessons is "showing" the child how to complete work, not just "telling" him.

There are hands-on materials included in almost every work. Once a lesson is presented a child can complete work without the need for verbal instructions or further communication with others. This can be very beneficial to a child with an auditory processing disorder or one who is sensitive to noise.

Montessori materials are typically made of wood, glass or other natural substances. They make minimal noise, unless designed to do so. Learning objects created from natural materials eliminates potential for over-stimulation that can occur with noisy battery operated items.

The Silence Game is designed to help with self-regulation in the classroom. The child practices being still and quiet for a specific period of time to improve concentration and awareness skills. Visuals and materials can be provided to help a child remain regulated and calm when necessary. The game can be used for individual students or can be practiced as a class.

The Peace Corner can be used whenever a child needs to take a break from auditory stimuli. It is a small space created in the Montessori classroom away from others, that promotes the ideas of peace, reflection and self-regulation. It usually includes a table with chair(s), and a few small items to represent peace, that will help the child self-soothe and calm down.

The Peace Corner can also be used for peaceful conflict resolution between students. Two children sit across from one another and express their feelings and concerns in a peaceful manner. An item can be handed back and forth as the two children take turns speaking.

The Peace Corner was not designed or recommended by Maria Montessori, but was later added to the curriculum to help promote Peace Education.

A child who craves auditory stimuli can have needs met as he is encouraged to spend as much time outdoors as possible. Time outdoors provides access to natural auditory stimuli along with the freedom and space to create noise without disrupting others in close quarters.

Tips for the Montessori Teacher

1. If a child with special needs requires more interventions related to auditory stimuli in the classroom, consider the following ideas.

    -Give the child sound blocking headphones to wear.

    -Let the child enjoy preferred sounds or music using headphones so as not to distract others who are   working.

    -Add visual cues and hands-on materials that require minimal verbal instructions to help the child through daily routines.

-Use auditory transition cues such as sounds or songs that draw the child's attention and prompt him to transition into another part of the daily routine, causing less confusion and disruption.

-Create a sensory-oriented anxiety kit with items that provide calming auditory input to be used when needed. Consider placing the kit close to the Peace Corner or near the door to be used outside.

-Help the child avoid situations that involve intense or unusual auditory stimuli which might be overwhelming or upsetting.

Behaviors

Managing and improving behaviors of a child with special needs is of the utmost importance for everyone involved. This is easier said than done. Every child with special needs is different, even those with the same diagnosis.

In order for a child to be successful in any learning environment, the teacher must understand the child's behaviors. As mentioned in one of my favorite books, *Uniquely Human* by Barry M. Prizant, all behaviors have purpose. Once a teacher understands the meaning behind the behaviors, she can provide supports necessary for him to be successful. But how does the teacher do that?

The ABCs of Behavioral Analysis

As parents of four special needs children, my husband and I have attended several trainings over the years. One of our favorites was a course presented by the Autism Treatment Network. The network works hand in hand with the hospital where our children are seen regularly.

As part of this training, we were taught the ABCs of Behavioral Analysis. This process has helped us significantly in developing ways for our children to be successful in the home and classroom environment.

A is for the Antecedent

What is happening right before the behavior occurs? In other words, what was the trigger? Here are some questions for the teacher to ask herself.

- Was someone talking to the child or asking a question?
- Was the child in transition?
- Did someone do something to the child?
- Was the child trying to communicate something to you or someone else?
- Was the child just exposed to certain types of sensory stimuli?
- Has the child been hurt?
- Was the child working through emotions?
- Was the child exposed to a trigger related to past trauma?

Take time to analyze each situation. Break situations down into observable, measurable actions. Record the events leading up to the undesired behavior. If there is no obvious antecedent for a behavior or if the child responds inconsistently to a specific antecedent, ask the parent about behaviors at home. Learn more about the child's physical, mental, emotional, and psychological state.

Sometimes, an explosive behavior may seem to arise out of nowhere because the child is still worked up over something that happened earlier in the day or an event in the more distant past. This information can help the teacher look for warning signs before things escalate, providing time to choose an appropriate response to the behavior.

B is for the Behavior

How is the child responding to the antecedent? What is the child doing? Negative behaviors a teacher may see include but are not limited to:

- Hitting
- Kicking
- Biting
- Thrashing
- Rolling around
- Screaming
- Yelling
- Throwing things
- Breaking things

Once the teacher connects the behavior with the antecedent, she can begin to identify patterns. These patterns can help the teacher decide how to intervene. She might teach a child different coping mechanisms and ways of communication that are more productive. Or she can also make modifications to the physical environment that might prevent the antecedents from occurring.

If a teacher is working with a child who is particularly challenging , she can use the ABCS of Behaviors Analysis to chart positive behaviors and earn what makes the child comfortable and happy. Over time the teacher will see patterns that will help her know how to make learning experiences more positive.

C is for Consequence

The consequence is the way in which an adult responds to the behavior. The teacher should consider the following questions when choosing a consequence.

- Is my response helping or hindering the child's success?
- What need is the child trying to fulfill through the behavior? Is he getting what he wants?
- Am I responding consistently and accurately to what's going on?
- Is my response reinforcing the behavior or am I working to manage it?
- Does the child understand the consequence?

The teacher's response to the child's behavior ultimately determines how the situation is resolved. Choosing consequences that help the child meet his needs without reinforcing the negative behavior is key. If the consequence is appropriate, the child will have learned something new and feel empowered to do better. If the consequence is given inappropriately or reinforces the negative behavior, no progress will be made.

Documenting the ABCs of Behavioral Analysis has affected our home and classroom for the better, more than any other intervention we've tried. If the teacher understands the needs and the struggles of the child, she can develop ways to help him.

Take the time to document each time a behavior occurs, using the ABCs of Behavioral Analysis for at least two weeks in the classroom, if not more. Look for patterns. Once patterns are identified, create a behavior plan that will help the child be successful. If the teacher can not find patterns and responses that are inconsistent at best, it's time for further investigation into the emotional health of the child.

The teacher may notice three main reasons why the child responds to situations in the way that he does. These include:

- Inability to communicate appropriately
- Transitions
- Noncompliance (The child refuses to do what's asked of him.)

Inability to Communicate Appropriately

A child with special needs may lack the ability to communicate appropriately in social situations. Instead of using words in response to the action of another, a child may hit, kick, bite, or scream.

When a teacher observes these occurrences and notices patterns using the ABCs of Behavioral Analysis she can begin to provide resources for the child with special needs to help him be successful when communicating with others. As the child learns to communicate effectively, behaviors will diminish and everyone involved feels successful.

Transitions

A transition is the time between the end of one activity and the beginning of another. A child with special needs may struggle with transitions, resulting in some pretty significant behaviors.

As the teacher analyzes the child using the ABCs of Behavioral Analysis, she can observe where he has difficulties transitioning and put proper supports in place to help during those times. Supports may include timers, auditory prompts, a visual schedule, and structuring preferred activities after non-preferred activities to provide incentive and reinforcements. Over time, when proper supports are put in place, the teacher will see a decrease in behavioral issues.

Noncompliance

At times, a child with special needs may display inappropriate behaviors because he doesn't want to do what's asked of him. In these cases, it's extremely important to analyze what it is he doesn't like and respond appropriately.

If the requested task is something that's mandatory, it will be important that the consequence is consistent, appropriate, and does not reinforce the noncompliant behavior. Incentives and reinforcers may be necessary to help the child comply.

If the teacher has flexibility in what's asked, it's important to remember that the main goal of behavioral analysis is to help the child be successful. The teacher can alter her request to ensure that the child feels empowered with choices, while reducing his noncompliant behaviors.

Behaviors in a Montessori Classroom

The ABCs of Behavioral Analysis work extremely well in a Montessori classroom as the teacher is constantly observing the child and following his interests, abilities and desires related to learning. In many instances behaviors improve through simple modeling and explanations. This occurs as the teacher presents Grace and Courtesy lessons in the classroom.

Grace and Courtesy lessons consist of instructions on social etiquette, manners, and appropriate behavioral responses to various situations in the classroom as they arise.

Transitions are minimal in a Montessori environment, as the child selects his own work and completes tasks at his own pace. Required transitions within the classroom are routine and expected. Experiences outside of the classroom are planned in detail before they are carried out, providing opportunities to address difficulties with transition.

Noncompliance is also minimal in a Montessori environment as the child selects his own work. The Montessori classroom supports a child's need for control over his actions.

Tips for Montessori Teachers

1. It is important to remember that a child with special needs may not remember from day to day, or hour to hour what they are "supposed" to do regarding social skills and behaviors in the classroom. Grace and Courtesy lessons may need to be presented several times.

2. Grace and Courtesy lessons may require visuals and hands-on materials to help the child with special needs learn. Once a child knows what to do, applying that knowledge can be extremely difficult. He may require more prompts, visual cues, and/or hands-on materials in order to be successful.

3. The abilities of a child with special needs may change often based on issues with sensory stimuli, self-regulation, triggers, and more. A child with special needs may struggle to generalize skills. Don't assume that because a child did well with a concept one day, he'll do just as well the next. That's rarely the case. Be patient.

4. If a child with special needs struggles with noncompliance in the classroom, it's important to understand why the child is acting out. There are very few reasons why a teacher might run into this issue.

Here are a few questions to reflect on.

-Are works on the shelves boring or too easy?

-Are the works too difficult?

-Is the child over stimulated and/or unregulated?

-Has the child been triggered emotionally in some way?

-Is the child struggling with issues not related to the classroom such as problems at home, emotional disability, etc.?

5. If a child has been triggered emotionally, preferred activities may help. If not, try time in the Peace Corner with preferred sensory stimuli until the child is calm.

6. The teacher may continue to find unexplained difficulties with non-compliance if the child has a mood disorder or a trauma based disorder. In these cases, constant communication between the parent and teacher is crucial. At times medical intervention will be necessary. Once the child is stable, success is possible in the Montessori classroom setting. It just may take far more time than the teacher would like.

Chronological and Cognitive Age

Chronological Age

The chronological age of a child is determined by his birthdate. It is how old the child is in years. When determining which grade level a child should be in, chronological age is the first matter of consideration with a typical child. In most cases the chronological age will match up with the cognitive, developmental, and emotional age of the child.

By contrast, the chronological age is the very last detail to take into account when deciding where a child with special needs should be placed. Differences between chronological, cognitive, developmental, and emotional ages in a child with special needs can be so great that placing him in a classroom only based on chronological age can be a recipe for failure.

A child with special needs develops differently than his peers. Most often there are delays in one or more areas. His skill set is lower. Expecting him to do more than he is capable results in significant behavior challenges.

Chronological Age in a Montessori Classroom

A child in a Montessori classroom learns alongside peers who are older and/or younger which can be very beneficial. If there are cognitive, developmental, and/or emotional delays or advancements, the child may still find works and materials in the classroom that are appropriate. When delays or advancements are more severe, a child can be placed in a Montessori classroom that best fits what he needs, at the teacher's discretion.

- The Nido (means nest) classroom includes children three to eighteen months of age.
- The infant/toddler classroom includes children eighteen months to three years of age.
- The preschool classroom includes children three to six years of age.
- The lower elementary classroom includes children six to nine years of age.

- The upper elementary classroom includes children nine to twelve years of age.
- The middle school classroom includes children twelve to fifteen years of age.
- The high school classroom includes children fifteen to eighteen years of age.
- Higher education includes children eighteen to twenty-four years of age.

Tips for Montessori Teachers

1. Spend time observing a child with special needs before deciding which classroom or curriculum would best meet his needs.
2. Discuss observations with parents and work together to find the best Montessori environment for the child that will enable success.
3. Do not assume that the chronological age of a child with special needs matches up with his classroom placement needs.

Cognitive Age

The cognitive age of the child is his ability to think and learn relative to his chronological age. This can be determined by IQ scores and/or other academic assessments. If a teacher does not have up to date scores for a child with special needs, she should request that testing be done. Scores are crucial to understanding the abilities of the child and what the teacher can expect in the classroom.

Tests must be done by a qualified professional. Different tests may be used in different countries. If testing is not covered by insurance or other medical provisions funding may be available through the school.

Understanding the cognitive age of a child can help eliminate several unnecessary behavioral issues. If a child has cognitive delays or an intellectual disability and the work is too demanding, he will act out. On the other hand, a teacher may find that a child is cognitively advanced. If classroom work is too easy, the child will become bored and the teacher may see behavioral issues. Both situations are completely avoidable.

When a child has a severe to moderate intellectual disability, lower test scores will be seen in every subject area across the board. The same is true of a child who is cognitively advanced. In general, he should perform about the same in math skills as he does in language and writing skills. In the case of specific intellectual disability, such as a math disability, scores on computational sections of the test will be significantly lower than scores on the verbal/language sections.

Once a child is eight years of age chronologically, IQ stays relatively stable over his lifetime. A child with an IQ score between 40 and 70 is deemed intellectually disabled. An IQ score of 70-79 is considered borderline intellectual functioning. The "normal" range is 85-115. Genius level IQ scores include those of 130 or more.

Cognitive Age in a Montessori Environment

A Montessori classroom can be the perfect place for a child with cognitive delays or advancements. There is a variety of materials and works available to meet the needs of the child, due to the age range of those in the classroom.

A child with special needs in a Montessori classroom goes at his own pace, choosing his own work. The teacher is expected to follow the child by providing materials that are consistent with his interests, in order to help the child reach his fullest potential. As long as the work on the shelves is cognitively age appropriate, a child with cognitive delays, an intellectual disability, or who is cognitively advanced can and will succeed at his own pace.

Most work in a Montessori environment comes with visual and tactile components that aid in the learning process, helping the mind and body connect. A child with cognitive delays or intellectual disabilities excels in ways he could not otherwise, due to the emphasis on experiential, rather than language-based, learning methods.

It is through the Montessori Method and materials that Maria Montessori was able to teach children who were otherwise considered unteachable. When Montessori's "unteachable" students were evaluated by state education officials, their scores were equal to their peers who were taught using the traditional methods of the day. This was a stunning achievement. That success can be repeated by today's special learners using those same methods and materials.

Tips for Montessori Teachers

1. Be sure to provide Montessori materials and works that match the cognitive abilities of the child. This may mean activities far below or above the child's chronological age.

2. If a child is cognitively more than two years older or younger than their chronological age, choose the Montessori curriculum that best fits where the child is at cognitively.

Developmental Age

The developmental age of a child is determined by his ability to adapt to the world around him and apply knowledge using:

- The senses
- Fine motor skills
- Gross motor skills
- Communication
- Appropriate emotional responses

The child's developmental age can have significant impact on his ability to learn. A child with special needs often has developmental delays that prevent him from reaching his potential related to his cognitive and chronological age. Even if IQ scores are high, delays in developmental age can prevent progress in academic performance and abilities. Such is the case for a child who has autism spectrum disorder (ASD).

A child with developmental delays may be on target or advanced with some skills and subject areas but not with others. This same child may progress at a much slower pace than his typical peers.

If a teacher is worried about a child's development she can discuss concerns with parents and request testing. Developmental age can be determined by results of various adaptive tests including the:

- Vineland Adaptive Behavior Scales
- Adaptive Behavior Assessment System
- Diagnostic Adaptive Behavior Scale

A pediatrician or school psychologist can refer a child for testing by a qualified professional for accurate results and explanations of scores. These scores are extremely important when it comes to helping a child with special needs in an academic setting. Different tests may be used in different countries. If testing is not covered by insurance or other medical provisions funding may be available through the school.

Developmental delays are one of the main reasons a child with special needs fails to thrive in a learning environment. When a child is expected to function and perform above his developmental age significant behavioral issues are sure to follow. The child does not progress, and in some situations regression in overall functioning may occur.

Developmental Age in a Montessori Classroom

A child with developmental delays can easily thrive in a Montessori environment when provided with lessons, work, and materials that are appropriate to his developmental age. Classrooms include children of various ages for the child with special needs to observe and learn from. Help and assistance are available when needed.

A wide range of works in every subject area is available at all times to accommodate a child's strengths and weaknesses. The child's academic progress will not be hindered due to specific weaknesses in one area or another. Maria Montessori encouraged teachers to follow the child, so if the child wants to only focus on strengths for a specific period of time, that is okay.

Preliminary exercises in the area of Practical Life help a child with special needs develop skills necessary for success in other subject areas. If the child struggles with fine motor skills, these works will be available when the child is ready.

Planes of Development and Tips for Montessori Teachers

One last aspect of developmental age that is extremely important to discuss in a Montessori environment is Maria Montessori's Planes of Development. These planes are used to design curriculum, determine classroom placements, and how to best meet the needs of each child.

The Planes of Development refer to how a typical child develops. A typical child's chronological and developmental ages usually match up. Remember this is not the case with a child who has special needs. When referring to the Planes of Development use a child's developmental age to determine what he should be learning and how he will react to the world around him, especially in regards to adaptive skills.

Emotional Age

A teacher may notice a child's ability to function and respond to environmental stimuli is inconsistent. Perhaps the child exhibits mood swings and/or has irregular sleep patterns? All of this may indicate that this child is struggling with emotional disabilities. These may include anxiety and trauma based disorders or mood disorders.

Anxiety Disorders

A child who suffers from an anxiety disorder may display fight or flight responses to situations that cause distress. A teacher may see a child be overly clingy. There may be meltdowns and other troublesome behaviors, especially if the child is unable to communicate emotions and request help when feeling anxiety. A teacher will notice the child is not functioning at their regular level when in the midst of a panic attack.

When an anxiety or mood disorder is present, a child's strong emotional reaction to triggers can not be dismissed. Though they may seem over the top or bizarre in some cases, they are real to the child. If they are real to the child, behaviors caused by them are real to everyone.

A child with an anxiety disorder may be triggered instantly by something in the environment, or feel increased anxiety over time due to fear of the unknown or fear of something in the future.

The goal of the teacher and other caregivers is to help the child manage triggers and episodes. Once a child with anxiety feels safe, he is able to communicate his feelings adequately. A child with anxiety sincerely wants help feeling better. Over time a child can learn coping mechanisms and help soothe himself.

Trauma Based Disorders

Post Traumatic Stress Disorder (PTSD)

A child with PTSD will function well, until he is triggered by a sensory stimulus in the environment that causes a panic, frightened reaction. Usually the trigger is similar to or a reminder of a traumatic event the child experienced in the past. A trigger can be as simple as a sound in the classroom that sounds like a noise related to trauma experienced.

In some cases, however, the trigger does not have to be directly related to the traumatic event in any obvious way, but somehow it became entangled within the child's emotional memory of the event or aftermath of the event.

Once triggered, a child may go into a full blown PTSD episode, at which time the he will be unable to function, think rationally, and/or have control over his own actions. PTSD is a serious condition that can lead to death if not treated.

If a child has PTSD, it is extremely important for the teacher to communicate with parents on a consistent basis to discuss triggers, episodes, behaviors, and treatment plans. A safety plan for the child in the classroom may also be required.

For more information about PTSD in children and how to help them, refer to *Holidays and PTSD: A Parent's Guide to Survival,* a book written by my husband, a licensed mental health therapist and me.

Reactive Attachment Disorder (RAD)

A child with RAD will do whatever he needs to in order to feel safe. He can only trust himself, which means he will push away others trying to care, bond, or love him in whatever ways necessary.

Common behaviors include, but are not limited to:

- Destructiveness
- Vandalism
- Pathological lying
- Chronic stealing
- Hoarding
- Refusing to eat
- Gorging to the point of vomiting
- Manipulation
- Fire setting
- Cruelty to animals and children
- Self-injurious behaviors
- Sexual behaviors
- Sexual activity with other children

- Bestiality
- Angry rages
- Physical aggression
- Violence
- Verbal attacks and abuse
- Passive aggression

Significant behavioral issues in the classroom are common. The child resorts to these behaviors in an effort to protect himself, as any form of attachment to others literally feels life threatening.

Positive incentives and reinforcers do not work with a child who has RAD. Negative consequences may not have an affect on the child either. What could be worse than what he's already experienced? A child with RAD is an expert at provoking others to anger. Managing behaviors is extremely difficult as the child feels an absence of guilt and may appear to have no conscience at all.

The child also possesses the crazy ability to act perfectly normal and innocent when he wants to. This is referred to as "artificial charm." He is a professional at pinning others against each other. He is usually just as good at pinning blame for his crimes on others. The child with RAD has a desperate need to feel in control at all times. Whether it's through causing absolute chaos or being the center of a attention the child can easily manipulate a situation to gain that feeling of control.

A child with RAD most often has a target, commonly the gender as the caregiver that abused him or neglected him. A child with RAD may engage in the behaviors listed above only with the target, but be perfectly fine with others. As a teacher spends more time with the child, behaviors will escalate, no matter if the teacher is the target or not.

Mood Disorders

If a teacher has concerns about a child with a possible mood disorder, it is extremely important that the child with special needs be seen by a qualified medical professional for help. Mood disorders do exist in young children. The sooner the child is diagnosed the sooner he can receive the help he needs in order to be successful in any learning environment. In most cases medical intervention is necessary. A mood disorder is a medical diagnosis that requires medication.

An unmanaged mood disorder can wreak havoc on any learning environment, especially when the child is unable to keep himself safe. A teacher may notice that the child is unable to progress in his learning process if manic and/or depressive episodes are left unmanaged. At best his abilities and behaviors will be unpredictable.

Our developmental pediatrician explained to us that when a child with a mood disorder is manic, his IQ score drops 20 points. When working with a child who has a mood disorder and episodes are not managed, it's important to make sure that all work and materials are safe.

Emotional Age in a Montessori Classroom

When analyzing and addressing differences in chronological, cognitive, developmental, and emotional ages, issues with emotional age always come first. A child can not be successful in a classroom, until issues are addressed and proper supports and safety plans are put into place.

However, once support, safety plans, and an understanding of behaviors have been developed, a Montessori environment is perfect for a child with emotional disabilities. A child with emotional disabilities often crave control. A Montessori environment helps him achieve this as he chooses his own work, is provided with controls for each activity, and has his entire mind and body focused on the task with tactile components.

Maria Montessori did not believe in rewards or punishments. She believed that a child had an inner need to do productive work. No excessive praise is encouraged either. Compliments are given with emphasis on the child's work, not the child. A Montessori teacher also tries to give encouragement rather than praise.

For more information about the use of praise in a Montessori classroom I highly recommend reading Deb Chitwood's post about this subject on the blog Living Montessori Now at http://livingmontessorinow.com/a-montessori-approach-to-praise/.

Maria Montessori's beliefs about rewards, punishment, and praise are brilliant when considering the needs of a child with reactive attachment disorder. The child feels safe and in control. Any threat of attachment is minimal, which means the child will feel less of a need to act out.

Tips for Montessori Teachers

1. When working with a child who has an anxiety/trauma based disorder, or mood disorder, use The ABCs of Behavioral Analysis to document triggers, episodes, and successful ways to help the child feel safe again.

2. Consider using a sensory-oriented anxiety kit filled with items that calm the senses to help a child with anxiety and trauma-based disorders. The kit can be stored near the peace corner for easy access.

Fine Motor Skills

Fine motor skills are small movements of the hand, wrists, fingers and other body parts. A child with special needs may have delays in fine motor skills that affect their ability to function and be successful in a traditional learning environment. Occupational therapists and one-to-one aides are often brought in to help the child when necessary.

Unfortunately, occupational therapy sessions only last so long. One-to-one aides most often assist in pre-assigned tasks. There is usually no additional time for further development of fine motor skills in the classroom setting, especially when the child is already at an age when mastery of the skills is expected.

Most often occupational therapy focuses on writing skills once a child is in kindergarten. Life skills that do not affect academic performance are often overlooked.

Fine Motor Skills in Montessori Environment

In a Montessori infant, toddler, and preschool classroom, a child is working constantly to develop fine motor skills. Many materials and work put a direct emphasis on developing these skills. Even in early and late elementary classrooms this can still be the case. All work and materials require handling and manipulation, key components to building fine motor skills.

A child is constantly working to develop strength in his fingers and hands. The pincer grasp and writing skills are practiced in multiple subject areas, but are not required if a child is not ready. Maria Montessori's advice to follow the child is crucial when it comes to developing fine motor skills.

The progression of material and curriculum builds on fine motor skill development. Practical Life skills are emphasized first through preliminary exercises to ensure that the child is developing the abilities necessary to succeed in other areas. Preliminary exercises include but are not limited to the following work:

- Sponge transfer
- Spooning

- Scooping
- Tong transfer
- Eyedropper dots on dish
- Pouring rice
- Pouring water

Practical Life work continues and is similar to activities in occupational therapy. Once a child masters preliminary exercises he moves on to other Practical Life tasks. These include but are not limited to:

- Indoor and outdoor cleaning tasks
- Dressing frames that teach the skills of snapping, buttoning, zipping, buckling, hook and eye, lacing and tying
- Caring for plants
- Food preparation
- Sewing skills
- Work with tools such as screwdrivers, nuts, bolts, locks and keys

If a Montessori teacher notices a child is struggling with very particular fine motor tasks, she has the liberty of creating custom Practical Life work that helps to develop specific skills. Maria Montessori only advises that the tasks have a real world application.

If a child is unable to write or continues to show delays in fine motor development, these struggles will not hold him back from progressing in other subject areas. There are multiple lessons and work that require no writing component. minimal fine motor skills are necessary. Completion of the work still demonstrates competency or mastery of a skill related to various subjects.

Tips for Montessori Teachers

1. If a child has significant delays in fine motor skills, do not hesitate to select works from a curriculum that matches the child's skill set.
2. If it is observed that a child has significant struggles with fine motor skills, learning numbers, letters and sounds, yet displays skills that are average or above in other subjects, a teacher may be identifying a learning disability.

Gross Motor Skills

Gross motor skills are the abilities needed to perform tasks requiring large muscles such as walking, running, jumping, sitting, crawling and other activities. A child with special needs may have delays or disabilities in the area of gross motor skills.

If the child doesn't have delays he may struggle with issues related to staying still in a learning environment. There are times when you may see both ends of the spectrum in one child. Sadly most educational environments do not put enough emphasis on the development of gross motor skills.

Most often a child is required to sit at his desk for long periods of time. Physical education activities and recess are reduced if not completely eliminated from a child's daily schedule. Time spent outdoors is rare and does not provide enough sensory input to help a child with special needs regulate and be ready for learning.

Gross Motor Skills in a Montessori Environment

The Montessori learning environment is quite the opposite. Developing gross motor skills is essential to the child's education at home and at a school. A child is not required to sit at a desk when learning. He can choose to work on the floor or at a table. When selecting work the child moves freely about the classroom. Once finished he returns it. If he needs to stretch or receive sensory input, he can do this.

Montessori emphasized learning at home, in the classroom, and the outdoor environment. It is through movement that the child discovers himself and his abilities. Sufficient space in and outside of the classroom is provided to do this.

Maria Montessori developed specific work, such as "Walk the Line," that emphasizes the development of gross motor skills, balance and concentration. When participating in this work the child walks on a line on the floor in the shape of an ellipse, with one foot in front of the other. Variations include carrying various objects etc.

A child participates in Practical Life work that requires gross motor skill development as well. Some of these include sweeping and mopping. If a child needs to engage in gross motor activities, this type of work is available. Accommodations can easily be made for a child who is unable to participate in this work due to physical disability.

Even as an infant, the Montessori Method emphasizes the importance of freedom without the restraint of items that limit mobility, such as a crib, high chair, etc. Montessori infant classrooms are filled with items that encourage gross motor development and freedom of movement. As one might guess, an infant with special needs thrives here as he is able to focus on skill development without the hindrances of modern day items deemed as "necessities."

A Tip for Montessori Teachers

1. If a child has significant delays in gross motor skills, do not hesitate to select works that promote gross motor development from a curriculum that matches the child's skill set.

Home Environment

Most educational settings vary from home environments. The focus of teaching between the two locations tends to be different. Activities and entertainment are altered. Conversation fluctuates as the role of the adult and child changes. At times, depending on circumstances, the contrast between the two locations is so huge, the child feels as if he is living in two different worlds.

A child attending school bridges the gap between the environments by bringing home assignments to be completed after school hours and possibly signed by a parent or guardian. Parents may help the child study for quizzes and exams. Books are sent home to read. There are also projects that require parental assistance.

The after school tasks mentioned above may cause conflict, behaviors and stress in the home, especially with a child who has special needs. Tasks are time consuming and take away from quality time that could be spent:

- Outdoors
- Developing better relationships with family members, friends and neighbors
- Learning a new skill
- Advancing hobbies
- Resting
- Exercising

Instead the time is spent completing educational tasks after already spending several hours in the classroom learning and practicing those skills.

How the Home Environment is Affected
by a Montessori Classroom

The Montessori Method was designed for the home and classroom. For a family who embraces Montessori, it isn't just a way to educate a child, but a way of life. Implementing Montessori principles at home can be extremely beneficial for parents who have a child with special needs. The continuity eliminates transitions and adjustments that are unnecessary. Expectations and methods of dealing with behaviors remain consistent.

There are no quizzes or exams in a Montessori classroom. No homework is sent home. All assignments and projects are finished at school. Time at home is dedicated to family and other activities. This difference alone eliminates so many unnecessary behaviors and meltdowns in a child with special needs. The brain is given permission to rest, which is necessary for success in both environments.

But just because Montessori education materials aren't in the home, doesn't mean that a family can't implement other aspects of the Montessori Method to provide continuity at home and at school.

Many families who adopt Montessori principles choose to implement them from the very moment a child is born or arrives through adoption. Starting early is ideal, but it's never too late to receive some benefits from Montessori principles at home. It doesn't matter what age the child is when you start.

Montessori at home encourages independence and self-sufficiency. It builds confidence and focuses on life skills which are necessary for success at every age. As a parent learns how to respond to behaviors using a Montessori approach, combined with the ABCs of Behavioral Analysis, the atmosphere will invite peace and respect for everyone.

There are several resources available for those interested in adopting the Montessori approach at home. Here are some of my favorite books to recommend:

- *The Joyful Child: Montessori, Global Wisdom for Birth to Three* by Susan Mayclin Stephenson
- *Montessori from the Start: The Child at Home from Birth to Age Three* by Paula Polk Lillard and Lynn Lillard Jessen
- *Understanding the Human Being: The Importance of the First Three Years of Life* by Silvana Quattrocchi Montanaro
- *Montessori Baby Guide* by Stacy Sanders
- *The Absorbent Mind* by Maria Montessori

- *How to Raise an Amazing Child the Montessori Way* by Tim Seldin and Vanessa Davies

A Tip for Montessori Teachers

1. If the child responds well to specific aspects of Montessori that can be applied to the home, don't hesitate to communicate this information to parents. Parents of a child with special needs love to hear about how their child is being successful and may apply concepts at home, which is a win-win for everyone.

Incentives and Reinforcers

For parents who are raising a child with developmental disabilities, especially ASD, incentives and reinforcers are crucial to success. An incentive is something positive that motivates a child to complete a task. Incentives are different from rewards in that the child knows what the incentive is ahead of time. A reinforcer is a positive response to a behavior that's been requested of the child.

It has been proven that a child who suffers from trauma related issues and/or untreated mood disorders does not respond to incentives and reinforcers. With trauma-related disorders, such as RAD, the trigger that provokes the behavior is stronger than any incentive could be. The child with RAD resists giving up control, even for something desirable.

Manic episodes and severely depressed episodes are also unreceptive to positive reinforcement. The "motor" that generates the manic behavior is dead-set on whatever it wants to do at the moment, completely uninterested in whatever a teacher has to offer. The depressed mood leaves the child with such low energy and motivation that no incentive would be powerful enough to shake it off. At times it's completely beyond the control of the child to remedy.

Incentives and Reinforcers in a Montessori Environment

Maria Montessori discouraged the use of external incentives and reinforcers. She believed that motivation to complete a task came from within the child. In her view, the satisfaction, confidence, and pride that results from successfully completing a task, without help, is it's own reward. This is of greater value than any token or verbal praise could ever be.

All aspects of the Montessori environment are designed with this principle in mind. Materials are beautifully arranged on trays and shelves. The child selects work based on his desire to complete it, not as a means to earn something else. Montessori materials and activities are the incentive.

Yet, there still may be a child who may lack the self-control or concentration level to find Montessori work rewarding all the time. Fortunately, a Montessori teacher has options.

When there is flexibility to create works based on the interests of the child, these can be used as incentives. If the child sees work about a subject or interest that he enjoys, he's more apt to select it from the shelves and complete it. But again the work is the incentive.

The child may have a passion for numbers and only select math work from the shelves. As Montessori counseled, the teacher has the flexibility to follow the child. If the child craves math, give him more math! The teacher can also incorporate numbers into other subject areas through sequencing work, etc. But just like in the examples above the work are still the incentive.

In a Montessori classroom reinforcers come in the form of controls within each work task and through the successful completion of it. A control allows the child to self-correct without the teacher's assistance. The child feels pride in what he has done. He selected a task and completed it on his own. Now he is motivated to try another.

A Tip for Montessori Teachers

1. If a teacher notices that a child with special needs loves a specific work task or material on the shelves, use it as an incentive or reinforce when necessary.

Juggling Multiple Special Needs

There are some children with special needs who carry a long list of diagnoses. Multiple diagnoses complicate a child's ability to learn in significant ways. For some, symptoms can be so severe that learning may not be possible at times. Ways to help are complicated for parents, teachers, and medical professionals. Progress with behaviors can be extremely slow.

These obstacles don't mean that academic progress is never possible. The time just may not be right yet. There is an order in which a child's special needs must be addressed at home and in an academic environment in order for success to be possible.

1. Physical/Medical Disabilities
2. Emotional Disabilities (Mental Health Issues)
3. Developmental Disabilities

Physical Disabilities

A child who is ill does not attend school. Whether it be due to the flu or a debilitating disorder that requires hospitalization, one would not expect a child who is suffering from these types of ailments to be successful in a classroom with other children. In these cases, alternative arrangements are made or education is put on hold until the child recovers.

Once the child is healthy again and able to learn, the child returns to the academic setting and progress resumes. A child who has missed a significant amount of time at school, may become overwhelmed trying to "catch up" Another child may experience temporary or permanent delays or changes in his ability to learn. But the way in which a teacher moves forward with their education is quite simple.

If the child is unable to attend school due to medical complications, a parent can consider homeschooling using a method or curriculum of choice and go at the child's pace.

Emotional Disabilities

A child with emotional disabilities may require medical intervention in order to be successful in a learning environment. As stated earlier in this book, without medical intervention the child can not progress and will not be successful in the classroom. The behaviors will be too extreme to ensure the safety of others and the child himself. However, once a child is stable, there is no reason why he can't be successful in a learning environment, unless there are other issues going on that also need to be addressed.

A child with trauma and/or anxiety issues may also need medical interventions in order to be successful in a learning environment paired with therapy and constant communication with parents and the child's team of specialists. Behaviors may be significant in these cases, and some healing may need to occur before a child can be successful, but it is possible.

If a child requires more time before he's ready to enter an academic setting with success, it's okay. It's better to be safe than sorry.

Developmental Disabilities

Once physical disabilities have been addressed, and emotional disabilities are stabilized, the teacher can begin to tackle issues related to developmental disabilities. The teacher's ability to manage situations that arise and how they affect others in the classroom, will determine if the child can be successful in the classroom environment. There are times when behaviors may be too severe to handle in the moment, but after therapy and medical intervention, are more manageable over time.

The child may need extra one-to-one support. Behaviors change with age and intervention. Just because a preferred academic setting isn't possible now, doesn't mean that it won't be possible later. All behaviors have meaning, so a child who is acting out is clearly stating that he is not ready yet.

Until the child is ready, consider a homeschooling option that allows the parent to go at the child's pace and make room for necessary therapies and other interventions. If circumstances are such that this is not possible, and the child is of an age where school is required, try to find the least restrictive environment in which the child and others around him can be safe, as you wait for him to be ready for better things in the future.

Juggling Multiple Special Needs

in a Montessori Classroom

A child with multiple special needs can be successful in a Montessori classroom when the teacher, parents and team of specialists are doing everything in their power to help the child. It is crucial to have as much documentation as possible about behaviors, along with cognitive and adaptive test scores.

There may be times when disabilities become unstable again, and a child may not be able to function. Once these issues are resolved, there should be no reason why the child can't return.

If a child has no diagnoses, yet there are concerns about severe behaviors in the classroom, parents should then pursue cognitive and adaptive testing. Scores acquired can confirm or deny fears, and if nothing else, help the parents and teacher better understand the needs of a child and how they can be addressed in a Montessori classroom. If further psychological assessments need to take place, they can now occur.

This process can be slow. All parties must try to remain calm and patient. If the child's behaviors become too difficult to mange in the classroom without the proper supports, the child may need to find an alternative academic setting until all information is available and a treatment plan has been made. But again, these are only temporary steps to help the child be successful in the long run.

If a parent insists that a child receive a Montessori education, even during these times, homeschooling using the Montessori Method is always an option. If the teacher is willing, she may help and guide the parent as they take on this responsibility at home until matters are situated.

Tips for Montessori Teachers

1. In situations with a child who has multiple special needs, it is crucial to use the ABCs of Behavioral Analysis to help with understanding the child and sort through which behaviors are related to which disability or challenge.
2. If a teacher notices inconsistencies in the child's level of functioning and ABC patterns on a regular basis, resulting in significant behavioral issues, she can discuss documented results and concerns with par-

ents and make a plan with them regarding steps that both take to help the child. If parents are unwilling to follow through with steps they need to attend to (which may include appointments with medical professionals and other specialists), the child will be unable to make progress. At times you may need to ask the child to leave until matters are resolved. But again this should only be temporary.

3. Please remember that a child with multiple diagnoses is the same type of child that Maria Montessori worked with when she began her medical career. Her observations and interventions with the children of Rome's asylums and orphanages were the foundation upon which she built her educational philosophy. This type of child is teachable and she proved this. The Montessori Method is set up to work for children with multiple diagnoses, and in most cases, is their only chance at success. The journey may be extremely difficult and tiresome but it is worth it, especially to the child and his parents.

Kid Safety

A child with special needs may lack safety awareness, have frequent meltdowns, rages, and/or outbursts of physical aggression. These behaviors can put the child and his peers at risk of being hurt.

In these instances it is important once again to observe and document the ABCs of Behavioral Analysis. In most cases, once the behaviors are understood, they can be minimized if not completely eliminated. If the behaviors do not subside, inquiries into further testing may be necessary to determine the issue and most often can be traced back to some untreated emotional disabilities or psychiatric problems.

Kid Safety in a Montessori Classroom

Maria Montessori felt it very important to use natural items in the classroom that were beautiful. This included glass items. One might think this presented some significant safety issues, but the very opposite occurred. The children enjoyed the items. They used them carefully and respectfully. Beautiful items in the classroom can help a child feel better about himself and thus encourage responsibility. He shares this responsibility with his peers, not just with the teacher.

Traditional Montessori materials are made of solid, natural materials. This makes them more durable, harder to destroy and enhances the child's ability to stay safe while working. The materials themselves help calm the child as they provide sensory input that he needs when transferring and in use.

The Montessori Method encourages a child to use sharp tools and other objects at a very young age, compared to today's standards. This may be concerning to some parents, especially those with a child who has special needs, but the result of introducing these tools earlier actually helps the child learn to use them safely. A teacher supervises until she feels comfortable that the child can be safe on his own.

These activities help the child feel responsible. They teach awareness and independence which minimizes risky behaviors in the long run. Lastly, they encourage fine motor development and provide sensory input the child may be needing. The child feels capable and confident.

Tips for the Montessori Teacher

1. Take the time to observe a child that is exhibiting unsafe behaviors. These behaviors have purpose. If identified and examined, in most instances they can be eliminated after careful behavioral analysis techniques have been used.

2. There are children, especially those with diagnoses like reactive attachment disorder who may exhibit self-harming behaviors or those dangerous to other children in the classroom. Work closely with parents and their team of specialists to determine what is best for the child. Close supervision during work tasks may be required.

3. Grace and Courtesy lessons can significantly improve the child's ability to be safe in the classroom, however the teacher must remember what was discussed about this process earlier in this book.

4. The Montessori mat or rug is used for working on the floor. It can be a fabulous tool when teaching a child with special needs about personal boundaries and safety awareness.

5. The Montessori Peace Corner can be a safe place for the child to go when the teacher notices he is agitated or escalating in behaviors. This is not to be done as a negative consequence or punishment, but instead as a positive way to help the child recognize his emotional state and learn to calm down before losing control. Be sure the Peace Corner is designed to be safe for a child with destructive tendencies.

Lessons

A child with special needs often struggles to understand lessons being taught in an educational setting and at home, especially when they are presented verbally without visuals and manipulatives. Difficulties with comprehension intensify when the child suffers from auditory processing issues, intellectual disabilities, is easily distracted, or lacks the ability to communicate questions appropriately.

When asked to complete assignments based on lessons the child does not understand, a teacher may encounter significant behaviors. The child is trying to communicate confusion and frustration. At times the child may be asking for help in the best way he can, even though it may be inappropriate.

In many educational setting, children are taught in large groups. This is especially unfortunate for a child with special needs. Large groups can add extra sensory stimuli that may distract him. The teacher may not have time to answer all questions. She also will not know if concepts are mastered until a child completes an assignment and she grades it.

Lessons in a Montessori Classroom

A Montessori teacher presents a lesson to a small group of students or an individual student. Small group size is very beneficial to a child with special needs. Lessons are presented in three periods.

1. The teacher presents the work to the child explaining it using words such as, "This is…"
2. The teacher then asks the child to explain what they've learned using words such as, "Show me…" This part of the lesson is very detailed to make sure the child is confident in what he has learned.
3. Lastly the teacher asks the child a question in relation to the activity such as, "What is this?" to ensure understanding.

Most lessons include visuals and/or manipulatives, which provide the child with sensory input he needs while at the same time helping the mind and body to connect while learning. Work tasks include a control of error which allows the child to identify and correct his own mistakes without assistance from the teacher.

All of these factors aid in the development of independence, self esteem, and confidence. A child is able to work on his own due to the control of error, once he has completed all three periods of the lesson successfully.

Lessons are presented in order of sequence outlined in the Montessori curriculum. Some Montessori teachers strictly follow this sequence. Others assert that there is some flexibility in the curriculum, if there is a desire from the child to learn about a particular material out of order, or if the teacher feels the child can benefit from learning an aspect of the activity early. At the same time a teacher may go backwards, if the child is lacking an understanding presented in a previous lesson and activity.

Tips for Montessori Teachers

1. Lessons may need to be presented several times to a child with special needs as his ability to perform in a learning environment may vary greatly from day to day, hour to hour, or minute to minute for a variety of reasons. Creating a visual sequence of steps for each activity may help the child with this.

2. A child with special needs may need individual steps of an activity broken down into smaller steps in order to follow directions correctly.

3. Smaller steps should be explained using as few words as possible, paired with a visual or manipulative component.

4. A child with special needs may have difficulties following the steps in the three period lesson. If this is the case, provide visual prompts for each period, so the child can understand what's going on.

5. A child with special needs may struggle answering questions. If a teacher notices a child with special needs struggling with period three of the lesson, it may be because he is unable to verbally articulate his answer, not because he doesn't know the material. A teacher can try to ask the question in a different way or return to period two of the lesson.

Materials and Manipulatives

Materials are tangible objects that one can touch, hold, and manipulate. A child with special needs often requires materials to aid in the learning process. Materials used for this purpose are often called manipulatives in the special needs world. Most are related to a lesson being taught to improve focus and concentration.

Materials and Manipulatives in a Montessori Environment

Manipulatives in a Montessori environment are Practical Life activities that require hand-eye coordination and meet the child's need for purposeful work.

Montessori materials are tangible objects that a child can touch, hold, and manipulate. They are used to aid in the learning process and to improve focus and concentration. Materials are necessary for the completion of Montessori work.

A Tip for Montessori Teachers

1. Become familiar with vocabulary related to special needs services, particularly language that will be included in reports about a child in the classroom. Understanding differences in word usage can be extremely helpful when executing plans in the classroom.

Nonfiction

A young child with developmental disabilities such as autism spectrum disorder (ASD), may show a particular interest in nonfiction entertainment such as encyclopedias and documentaries about his favorite subjects. These subjects can become all consuming, but also can provide comfort to the child when he is distressed.

Obsessions can serve as a way for the child to self-soothe. An intense interest in non-fiction topics such as astronomy, dinosaurs, or medieval warfare can pave the way towards a career in adulthood.

The same child with ASD may struggle with make-believe ideas and fairy tales. These concepts may be too abstract and therefore confusing. Fictional entertainment may be too nonsensical and therefore causes distress, especially as the child with ASD is struggling to understand the world around him.

As the child grows older, he still may prefer nonfictional forms of literature and entertainment but will probably branch out into the fictional world, too. However, it is at this time that the child may begin to develop the habit of slipping into the all-consuming fictional world to self-soothe.

Obsessing about *Harry Potter* or *Lord of the Rings*, at the expense of learning new academic concepts, can hinder a child's educational progress. Drawing the child's attention to non-preferred topics becomes more difficult, precisely when concepts are more advanced and require more concentration and effort. The potential for disaster is easy to see.

The preference for nonfiction has major implications for other disorders as well. A child with a trauma or anxiety-based disorder may prefer to think about fictional ideas and stories to escape from the dark and scary realities of the world he perceives all around him.

This can be particularly dangerous when the child decides to disassociate himself from the real world, reverting to a world of fantasy to escape and not cope with feelings that need to be worked through in order for healing and progress to occur.

Underdeveloped emotional growth will quickly undermine a

child's academic progress and level of functioning in the classroom. It is easy to miss this as a cause of problems, since a teacher can't read a child's mind.

Nonfiction in a Montessori Environment

Maria Montessori believed that children under the age of six should only be exposed to nonfiction forms of entertainment. All pictures in books should be photographs or true-to-life illustrations. This was to help the developing mind know the difference between fantasy and reality. It also helps the child develop a better understanding of the world around him.

Since Montessori's time, this emphasis on nonfiction has been expanded to all forms of media and entertainment. Technology devices in general are discouraged until the age of six.

Opinions vary greatly among Montessorians when interpreting the words of Maria Montessori on this subject. Some believe that true to life books, meaning fictional books with stories and characters that are realistic, are okay to include in a classroom curriculum. Other teachers believe that books with illustrations rather than photos are okay. There are some Montessori teachers who believe that it is okay to expose children to fictional forms of entertainment with discussion about the difference between fantasy and reality.

For the purposes of this book, nonfiction in a Montessori environment is being discussed as it relates to the benefits of a child with special needs. Maria Montessori worked with these children and developed the curriculum based on her observations of their needs, which are consistent with discussions and various observations in the special education realm today.

Tips for Montessori Teachers

1. The recommendation of six years of age is based on the development of the child. A child with special needs may continue to need or prefer only nonfiction until he is cognitively, emotionally, and developmentally six years of age. Remember these ages differ from the chronological age of the child.

2. Only providing nonfictional materials in the classroom up until the

age of six years developmentally, may help a child remain in the present, rather than retreat to his imaginary world. This can allow better focus and functioning with a child who have a diagnosis of ADHD, a trauma-based disorder, or ASD.

Olfactory and Oral Stimuli

Olfactory Stimuli

A child with special needs may show extreme sensitivity to or crave olfactory stimuli. The olfactory system is the sense of smell. If a child is hypersensitive to smells, he may avoid situations and activities that feature them. He may also avoid a person who has a strong scent from lotion, perfume, detergent, coffee etc.

A child who has a history of significant trauma may be triggered by specific smells. Triggers can result in PTSD episodes and/or extreme behaviors. This child may be fine one moment and then the opposite in a matter or seconds.

A child who craves olfactory stimuli will be drawn to pleasing scents. At times this can lead to unusual and unsafe behaviors as well as a violation of personal boundaries. This child may need to be provided with extra ways to receive olfactory input such as items to smell when he is trying to self-regulate.

Olfactory Stimuli in a Montessori Classroom

Maria Montessori was acutely aware of a child's need for olfactory stimuli. She even included scented bottles in her Sensorial curriculum. This is an activity in which a child smells various bottles, matching up those that are the same.

The Montessori Method also focuses on helping the child become more aware of olfactory stimuli in nature. Fresh flowers and live plants are encouraged in the classroom. Exploration of scents is also encouraged outside of the classroom. Where it is possible, Montessori schools have gardens that the children tend, filled with different olfactory experiences. Fresh foods are also prepared in most classrooms.

Various scents may also be present while completing Practical Life activities such as polishing sliver, shining shoes, and washing a table using soap and water.

A child who is sensitive to olfactory stimuli always has a choice of activities in a Montessori classroom and therefore can avoid close contact with a scent if desired. The child can work to overcome sensitivities at his own pace without pressure.

Tips for Montessori Teachers

1. If a child is hypersensitive to olfactory stimuli the teacher may want to create a designated work space for all tasks that involve strong scents. She may also consider having a "safe zone" for the child when others are working with materials that involve undesired scents. If a "safe zone" is not possible, consider providing a natural item with a desired scent that the child can smell and keep close when needed.

2. If a child craves olfactory input, consider keeping an item with an enjoyable scent available to the child in the classroom at all times. This may come in the form of a plant or flower, a cinnamon stick, etc. When the child craves the scent to help self soothe, he can have access to it, thus eliminating the threat of escalating behavioral issues.

3. If a child has a history of trauma work closely with parents or guardians to obtain a history of the child's experiences and ask for any known sensory triggers. Put together a safety plan so that all are prepared to respond immediately and appropriately if needed.

Oral Stimuli

Just like with olfactory stimuli, a child with special needs may be extremely sensitive to oral stimuli, or the sense of taste. This child may avoid situations where he may be required to eat or taste certain foods. At times this sensitivity can result in behavioral issues related to meal prep, meal time, and special occasions that involve food.

For some with sensitivities to oral stimuli complete avoidance of food preparation areas is typical. Others may be able to prepare foods, but not eat them. Each child is very different. Oral sensitivities may be a result of the texture of the food, rather than the taste. Sensitivities to oral stimuli are very different than the picky eater phase, which is typical in a young child.

A child with a history of past trauma may be triggered by specific oral stimuli. Triggers can result in PTSD episodes or other significant behaviors. This child may be completely fine one moment and then the opposite in a matter of seconds. A child who has been neglected or starved may display bizarre behaviors related to oral stimuli. He may refuse food or overeat. The teacher may see gorging or vomiting. A teacher could also see stealing and hoarding behaviors.

A child with special needs may crave various types of oral stimuli unrelated to appetite. He may like to bite or chew or suck on things. The child is constantly putting food and non-food items in his mouth. He may crave specific textures or tastes, or simply enjoy the pressure on the jaws from biting down on something. Constant oral stimuli often needs to be provided to prevent unsafe or disruptive behaviors related to the needs of the child.

Lastly, it is very common for a child with special needs to also have special dietary needs. This could mean a child has food allergies, intolerances, or other medical conditions that affect what the child can eat. In these instances specific oral stimuli can pose a safety risk to the child.

Oral Stimuli in the Montessori Classroom

Oral stimuli are very prevalent in a Montessori classroom. Students engage in Practical Life work that involves food preparation techniques. Snacks and meals are part of the daily schedule, depending on the age of the child. Oral stimuli may also be included in the Sensorial curriculum.

Though oral stimuli is available in the classroom on a regular basis, a child who may be hypersensitive is not required to select Practical Life or Sensorial activities that involve food from the shelves. The child chooses his own work.

When it comes to presenting lessons and following the curriculum, there are several ways for a child to develop skills introduced in Practical Life with food activities, that don't require the use of food.

Montessori schools vary in that some require children to bring their own snacks and lunches, while others have children prepare food in the classroom as part of their day. In whichever case, the parents are able to communicate with the school about their child's special dietary needs and how they will best be met. Each school and circumstance will be different.

Tips for Montessori Teachers

1. Be sensitive to a child who may be triggered by oral stimuli in the classroom, whether it's snack time, meal time, or part of a work task. The teacher works with parents to set up safety plans for the child at certain times of the day or in certain areas of the classroom to help him be successful and feel safe.

2. If a teacher is working with a child who is hypersensitive to oral stimuli and avoids all activities that involve food, work with the parent to learn about foods the child does enjoy and how those can be tied into daily work in the classroom.

3. If a child has a very limited palette, a teacher can work slowly to help the child expand food choices by introducing similar oral sensory experiences. For example, if a child will only eat vanilla yogurt, slowly introduce other flavors that are the same color and consistency, if the child is motivated and has a desire to participate.

4. There are several inexpensive resources available for a child who needs to chew that can be used in the classroom and not distract from work. For more information, be sure to visit www.everystarisdifferent.com. Providing the oral sensory input the child needs will help with concentration and encourage success.

5. If a child is unable to participate in work that includes food due to special dietary needs or medical conditions, ask parents to provide safe food items so the child will not miss out. If this is not possible, try to provide alternative work that the child will enjoy.

Proprioceptive Stimuli

When a teacher thinks about the senses: sight, taste, touch, smell and sound, she sometimes doesn't realize that she's forgetting a couple others, one being the proprioceptive sense. A child with special needs may show extreme sensitivity to proprioceptive input or crave it.

Proprioceptive input is a sensation that is felt inside the body, specifically in muscles, tendons, and other tissues. A child who craves proprioceptive input usually likes a lot of deep pressure. He can obtain this from massages, weighted materials, physical exercise, pushing or lifting heavy objects and rough play, among other things.

Proprioceptive input varies from the sense of touch in that it is experienced inside the body, not through contact on the exterior surface.

In the classroom, both extreme sensitivity to and the craving of proprioceptive stimuli can be problematic. A child is required to sit at a desk for the majority of the day with minimal breaks for movement and exercise. A lack of proprioceptive stimuli can lead to significant behavioral issues that may be unsafe for the child and others around him.

Proprioceptive Input in a Montessori Classroom

A Montessori classroom is a great match for a child with intense needs for proprioceptive input. Movement is promoted and encouraged, both inside and outside of the classroom. A child chooses to work at a table or on the floor using mats or rugs. With each activity, the child selects work from the shelves, carries it to a chosen work space, and then returns it to the shelves when completed. Many work tasks require movement in order to be completed.

Some Montessori materials are quite heavy, providing substantial proprioceptive input. If a child is unable to lift a material on his own, he can ask for assistance from a classmate or teacher.

There are Sensorial works that are designed to provide proprioceptive input. These include the Pink Tower, Red Rods, and Brown Stair, which are all different shaped blocks of varying weights and sizes. When a child is seeking this input, he can select this work from the shelves to self-regulate.

Proprioceptive input is also provided through several Practical Life activities including washing a table and sweeping. In some schools a children are responsible for the cleaning of the classroom which includes the movement of tables and chairs.

Outdoor exploration and movement is encouraged in a Montessori classroom as well, allowing a child to receive necessary proprioceptive input throughout the day, in a way that helps him focus better during work tasks.

Tips for Montessori Teachers

1. If a teacher notices a child who can't seem to get enough proprioceptive input, encourage as much movement and heavy lifting as possible during the day through work and materials.

2. If a teacher observes that a child needs even more proprioceptive input to stay regulated look into weighted items to have on hand for the child to use. Some of these items include: weighted vests, blankets, backpack and lap pads.

3. If a child is sensitive to proprioceptive input and avoids materials and work that require heavy lifting, help the child move materials to a table or rug or ask another child to assist them.

Questions

A child who has autism spectrum disorder (ASD) and/or other disabilities may struggle with answering questions. This is due to a number of reasons, including auditory processing issues, distractibility, inability to communicate verbally and/or social anxiety.

Difficulties answering questions can lead to significant issues while learning. The child may be unable to answer questions verbally or in writing. This is not because the child doesn't know the material. He may understand it perfectly and lacks the ability to communicate his responses correctly. .

Visual cues and hand-held materials can help a child to answer questions, but not in all situations. Difficulty answering questions can be the barrier that blocks a child from excelling in a learning environment.

Questions in a Montessori Environment

In a Montessori classroom, children are instructed using the three period lesson as discussed previously in this book. If you recall, the three period lesson includes the following dialogue components:

1. "This is…"

The teacher models the activity using the necessary Montessori materials, providing auditory and verbal instruction.

2. "Show me…"

The teacher encourages the child to demonstrate what the teacher has done. If the child is unable to do this, the teacher shows the child again. A child who struggles with communication issues can be confident as he shows his teacher how to do something. In a Montessori classroom, showing means doing, not always talking.

3. "What is this?"

Questions come last as the child is expected to demonstrate mastery of the skill. Mastery does not necessarily require verbal communication. The child can show his response without having to verbalize anything. At this point, both the child and the teacher are confident in the child's abilities, eliminating any anxieties the child may have. Because the child has already demonstrated the skill, and knows what's expected, auditory processing issues are negated. A child with limited verbal skills can model the skill, answering the question to everyone's satisfaction.

Tips for Montessori Teachers

1. For a child who struggles with communication in general, provide visual cues for each period of the lesson.

2. If the child can write, have him write down answers in the last period of the lesson when necessary.

3. If the child can not write, provide cards with possible answers for the child to choose from to demonstrate mastery.

4. If a child struggles working with a teacher due to social anxiety or fear of making errors in front of an authority figure, ask a classmate who knows the material well to work through the lesson with the child. The teacher can observe and determine if the child has achieved mastery.

Rotation of Materials and Activities

In many cases, a child with special needs enjoys consistency. He may tend to be rigid with his schedule and engage in ritualistic behaviors. As long as all aspects of the environment and schedule stay the same, the child will be relatively content. However if changes are made he may feel confused, agitated and anxious, which could possibly lead to behavioral outbursts.

A child who enjoys rigidity and ritualistic behaviors may choose the same activities day in and day out without variation. The child may engage in these behaviors to self soothe, regulate or to reduce anxieties. It can be very hard to deviate from these routines, depending on how long they have been in place and what need they provide for the child. Even minimal changes can trigger some pretty mean meltdowns.

Sometimes this rigid adherence to doing the same things the same way everyday can be so powerful that it inhibits the child's ability to move forward with his learning. This is not due to the child being intimidated or unfamiliar with the new materials; he is simply stuck. In these cases, it is important to shake up the routine to allow for new learning. Expect some degree of reluctance on the part of the child, but eventually confident and considerate prodding by a kind teacher will be accepted.

Rotation of Materials and Activities
in a Montessori Classroom

In a Montessori classroom, materials and work are kept on shelves. Some seasonal and lesson-specific materials are rotated regularly, but other work and materials usually remain on the shelves throughout the year. The permanence of these materials and work can be very comforting and beneficial for a child who does not like changes in the classroom.

Other work and materials on the shelves are usually rotated every few weeks to a month due to seasons, holidays, and the opportunity for all children in the classroom to learn and master materials presented. However a Montessori teacher is able to follow the needs of the child and change out work and materials on the shelves more or less frequently.

Tips for Montessori Teachers

1. If a teacher has a child who struggles with frequent rotation of materials and work, select a day of the week or month when the child can prepare and expect changes to be made. A teacher can prepare the child for the changes by explaining what he can look forward to.

2. If a teacher notices a child is stuck in a ritual, she can consider changing out the shelves more frequently. Be sure to advise the child ahead of time, to avoid the extra surprise factor that he is so keen to avoid. Eventually, the child will begin to anticipate the changes, thus offering reassurance in its routineness.

3. If a teacher notices that a child uses a particular activity or material to self-soothe when having difficulties, she may want to consider keeping it available for an extended period of time, as an incentive or reinforcer, or make it available upon request to be taken to the peace corner to help calm the child, if appropriate.

4. If a child is resistant to change to the point of showing extreme behaviors, consider taking baby steps by creating work and materials similar to preferred tasks, and placing them next to the other work.

Stimming and Self Regulation

Self-regulation is a child's ability to manage and control responses to sensory experiences and strong emotional situations. A child with special needs may struggle with self-regulation, due to:

- Sensory sensitivities and cravings that overwhelm his ability to stay regulated
- Difficulty understanding and managing strong emotions
- A lack of understanding social cues
- Unexpected changes in routine

When a child with autism spectrum disorder (ASD) feels anxious, excited, unregulated, fearful, or experiences strong emotions in general, he may engage in stimming behaviors. Stimming or self-stimulation is the repetition of physical movements of the body, sounds, and/or objects to help a child with ASD self-soothe. An example of a well known stimming behavior is hand flapping.

There are some who believe that stimming is not a good thing. It often appears bizarre or socially unacceptable. The repetitiveness may seem unhealthy or obsessive. Some view stimming as a target behavior that can be reduced or eliminated through behavioral interventions.

Others have recognized it's benefits, viewing it as a way for a child with autism to feel safe or self-regulate. If a child feels safe and regulated, his behaviors improve. Meltdowns and outbursts lessen. The child will begin to trust, open up, and progress in a learning environment.

Stimming can also be a way for a child to communicate how he's feeling. If a teacher observes the behavior, charting the ABCs of Behavioral Analysis, she may discover patterns that will help her understand how the child is feeling, even when he's not able to communicate these things verbally. Once the teacher understands the feelings the child is communicating she can help him in ways that he needs.

Stimming and Self Regulation in the Montessori Classroom

In a Montessori classroom, a teacher may notice that a child with autism or other developmental disability stims, trying to self-regulate.

This child may choose the same work over and over again. He may be drawn to a specific material and can't keep his hands off of it. The child may physically or verbally stim.

Stimming is okay as long as the child is:

- Being safe
- Using work and materials appropriately
- Not disturbing others
- Completing work in the classroom

The child is self-soothing and learning at the same time. Stimming can lead to extraordinary learning experiences if viewed as an interest rather than a behavioral issue.

The Montessori materials and work are intended to help a child self-regulate. They were designed based on Maria Montessori's understanding of the body's need for sensory experiences. Repetition is the key to being able to master any given work. This leads to focus and awareness. Students are encouraged to use materials in the classroom to help with self- soothing and self-regulation.

Tips for Montessori Teachers

1. Create a special spot in the classroom for the child to go when he needs to physically or verbally stim, so he will not disrupt others. The peace corner may be an ideal spot if set up correctly.

2. If the child stims on a material using it inappropriately, remove it from the learning environment if possible. Provide the child with an alternative material that's similar to the first, but better suits where the child is at developmentally.

3. If the child is stimming on a material that he has not been introduced to through lessons, but is using it appropriately, teach the lessons corresponding to the material. A child with developmental disabilities shows weaknesses in some areas but extraordinary strengths in others. The child may be communicating his readiness to learn in ways you did not expect. Remember to follow the child.

Tactile Stimuli

Tactile is another word for the sense of touch. In an environment there are several experiences related to tactile stimuli. A child may touch various objects or people. The child may be touched by various objects and people. Each time the child touches something or is touched he reacts differently depending on his ability to process sensory information.

Factors to consider when thinking about various responses to tactile stimuli include:

- Texture
- Temperature
- Water content (wet or dry)
- Various parts of the body have different responses than others

A child with special needs may be very sensitive to tactile stimuli. He may not enjoy being touched. When it comes to tactile stimuli around him, the child may have very specific preferences. A tactile experience that is not preferred will most often be avoided.

Another child with special needs may crave various types of tactile input in an environment. He may enjoy being touched and seeks out physical contact often. The child may crave various types of tactile stimuli and seek them out in the classroom and other environments.

Most needs related to tactile input can easily be met by removing tactile stimuli that the child is trying to avoid, or by providing tactile stimuli the child craves. The child will feel safe and regulated when his sensory needs are met in the classroom. Safety and self-regulation lead to fewer behavioral issues. When a child with special needs feels safe, he is more apt to try new things, more open to new experiences.

A child with special needs may require tactile stimuli to aid in the learning process. If a child is able to touch and use objects while learning, he may be better able to understand the concepts being presented. Hand-held objects used to aid in the learning process are called manipulatives in the special needs world, as discussed in a previous chapter.

Without manipulatives, a child with special needs may not be able to learn concepts that are presented orally and even visually. Appropriate tactile stimuli in the classroom can be the determining factor in a child's academic success.

Tactile Stimuli in a Montessori Classroom

Tactile stimuli in a Montessori classroom abounds. It is everywhere. Most Montessori work includes a tactile component. This provides opportunities for a child who seeks out tactile input, to receive it.

The child selects his own works from the shelves and is not required to touch or interact with any tactile stimuli he wants to avoid. Work is kept on shelves for easy viewing and selection. There are no surprises.

When it comes to contact with other classmates, a child works at a table or on a Montessori mat or rug on the floor. The child selects his own workspace and can move around if needed. The mat or rug on the floor is a visual reminder to others that this is the child's workspace. Others are not welcome unless invited.

These same concepts help the child who may crave tactile input as well. The child can select work from the shelves that best provides the tactile input he may need. The workspace, whether a table or rug can be a visual reminder to the child to respect other's personal boundaries, unless invited to join in.

Tips for Montessori Teachers

1. If the child prefers to avoid physical contact with other students and the Montessori rug is not a sufficient aid, provide a "safe" work spot for the child where he can feel safe and not have to worry about being touched by others.

2. If a child craves tactile input, keep a tray of objects with preferred sensory stimuli for the child to use when he can't resist touching things. The tray could be kept near the Peace Corner. When the child recognizes the need to touch things, he can go there to regulate without disrupting other students.

Unit Studies

The term "unit study" refers to a group of activities that have the same theme. This theme can be selected by the teacher or by the child. Unit studies are often used in educational settings to help the teacher organize curriculum. They can also be used as incentives to follow the interests of a child.

It is well documented that a child with autism spectrum disorder (ASD) or other developmental disabilities can be motivated by an incentive related to an interest the child has. If a child with ASD is obsessed with construction vehicles, there's a pretty good chance that if construction vehicles are used in a work activity, the child will want to participate, even if he does not prefer the learning task in general.

Designing work activities and materials around a child's interests is a great way to encourage learning and the development of other skills such as communication and social skills. A child with special needs will feel much more comfortable talking about an interest he has, rather than a nonpreferred subject given by the teacher.

Unit Studies in a Montessori Environment

The term unit study is controversial in the Montessori community. However all Montessori teachers I spoke with while conducting interviews for this book stated that they felt it extremely important to follow the interests of the child as Maria Montessori taught. Many also expressed a sincere desire to do all they could to help a child with special needs succeed in their classroom.

One way Montessori teachers can help a child with special needs is to create work tasks that appeal to his interests or obsessions. Montessori teachers often create work for the shelves in relation to a holiday, season, interest or other special occasion.

It would not be inconsistent with Montessori principles to create work tasks in each subject area that follow the intense interests or obsessions of a child with special needs so long as the interests are not based on fiction or fantasy. Often, works designed around a theme help with vocabulary development and other skills.

At times a child with special needs will show an intense interest in a preferred subject in a Montessori classroom. This obsession may be so strong that the child only completes work in this subject area for an extended period of time. This may last several days, weeks, or months depending on the rotation of the materials, the rigidity of rituals created by the child, and/or the self-soothing the works provide.

Viewed this way, a Montessori teacher can create works in other subject areas that tie in the intense interest or obsession creating a unit study of sorts, without varying from Montessori principles.

If a child is obsessed with Botany and will only complete Botany work in the classroom, a teacher can have the child add flowers or practice spelling the names of vegetables and fruits using the Montessori Moveable Alphabet. The child can study plants from around the world as part of cultural studies. Practical Life cutting activities could include cutting stems of flowers, transferring seeds, or scooping dirt.

Tips for Montessori Teachers

1. If a teacher observes a child in the classroom with an intense interest or obsession in a particular subject or theme, take advantage of the opportunity to encourage and inspire learning. Follow the child's lead and use the subject or theme to help him grow into other subject areas by designing works to supplement Montessori materials and principles.

2. Work related to a child's obsessions and intense interests can be used as incentives in the classroom when needed, to help motivate a child to work, when he is struggling.

3. Work related to a child's obsessions and intense interests can help a child self-regulate, focus and learn, thus improving behaviors in the classroom.

Vestibular and Visual Stimuli

The vestibular sense is less heard of, relating to the inner ear and the sense of balance. A child with special needs may struggle with vestibular input. Struggles with vestibular input can have an affect on how a child functions in a classroom setting.

If a child is hypersensitive to vestibular input he may prefer activities that allow him to keep both feet planted on the floor. He will avoid activities such as spinning, swinging, sliding or rolling. Yet, this same child may have an extraordinary ability to balance, and this is how he stays regulated.

A child who craves vestibular input will enjoy spinning, swinging, sliding and rolling activities. These kinds of activities are not usually offered in a classroom setting. If the need for vestibular input is not met, the child will seek it out any way he can. At times this can lead to unsafe behaviors.

A classroom environment where a child is expected to sit at a desk for several hours with minimal breaks for physical exertion is most likely not an environment where a child who craves vestibular input will thrive.

A classroom environment where a child is expected to be physically active, engaging in activities that stimulate the vestibular sense on a daily basis, is most likely not an environment where a child who is hypersensitive to vestibular input will thrive.

Vestibular Input in a Montessori Classroom

The Montessori environment is ideal for a child who is highly sensitive to vestibular stimuli. It is also ideal for a child who craves it. Montessori acknowledged these needs as she emphasized purposeful movement in the classroom.

A child is not required to stay seated throughout the day. He may complete activities standing up, sitting down or while laying on the floor if necessary. All of these positions help the child receive the appropriate vestibular input throughout the day.

The Montessori curriculum includes work that promotes the development of the vestibular sense including "Walk the Line." In this work the child practices walking on a straight line developing balance and posture. There are many variations to this work for children to enjoy and practice.

Maria Montessori encouraged the exploration of the outside world. Students spend time outdoors as often as possible. However, they are not required to use specific equipment or engage in specific work that is not preferred. Spending time in nature can benefit both those who are sensitive to and those who crave vestibular input as they can freely meet sensory needs and stay regulated.

Tips for Montessori Teachers

1. If you have a child who craves vestibular input, consider providing physical activity breaks for this child throughout the day. Once the child's vestibular needs are met, he will be able to focus and attend to tasks in the classroom.

2. A child who is hypersensitive to most kinds of vestibular input can be harder to identify in the classroom. The best tool is observation. If a work is introduced to the class that involves spinning, rolling, sliding, etc. and you see the child is more anxious or agitated than usual when engaged in the activity or watching others do the activity, this is a good moment to acknowledge what the teacher is seeing and remind the child that he is free to choose whatever work he would like. He is not obligated to do all of it.

Visual Stimuli

Visual stimuli refers to things that you can see in the environment. A child with special needs may respond differently to visual stimuli than his peers. He may have a vision impairment or suffer from blindness. The child may be extra sensitive to visual stimuli or he may crave it. In all of these cases the classroom environment can be challenging.

A child with a vision impairment or blindness will need hands on material to aid in the learning process. He will need sufficient space to move about without running into things or knocking something over. There will need to be consistent order and cleanliness in the environment in order for the child to function.

A child who is sensitive to visual stimuli will also require a consistently clean and orderly environment to function. The child may become overwhelmed easily when overstimulated by too many things, too much color, too much light, movement, etc.

A child who craves visual stimuli will seek out ways to fulfill that need. The child may enjoy watching items spin, fly through the air, scatter, etc. This child may enjoy dumping and building. He may also like knocking things down to watch them fall. The child may enjoy learning about colors, letters, numbers, and shapes, as these all provide various types of visual stimuli. This child may enjoy sensory bins, water play and weather, all due to the visual stimuli these learning activities provide.

Visual Stimuli in a Montessori Classroom

Maria Montessori encouraged learning environments to be clean and orderly. She encouraged open space to facilitate and invite movement throughout the classroom. Works and materials are organized on shelves for easy access and viewing, or feeling if need be. Most lessons and work include hand-held materials that can easily be manipulated for a child who has a visual impairment or suffers from blindness.

A child who is sensitive to visual stimuli can benefit from the cleanliness and order a Montessori classroom environment provides. Natural materials within the environment provide a sense of calmness, without being overwhelming both inside and outside of the classroom. Beauty is encouraged in it's most simplistic form.

A child who craves visual stimuli will also thrive in a Montessori environment as materials and works are designed to appeal to the eye. Many of Maria Montessori's materials have a visual component, whether it's a shape or color. This visual component reinforces concepts taught verbally and through hands-on experiences with materials.

Tips for Montessori Teachers

1. If a child is extra sensitive to visual stimuli in the classroom and/or outdoors, consider providing the child with sunglasses to help.
2. If a child visually stims on work and materials, remember this is encouraged so long as the child is being safe, using activities and mate-

rials appropriately, not disturbing others and completing work in the classroom.

3. If the child is visually stimming in unsafe and unproductive ways, remove materials from the classroom if possible. If not, provide the child with alternative developmentally appropriate work that is similar to the stimming task.

4. If a child requires more visual stimuli than provided in the classroom and in the natural outdoor environment, consider creating a tray of visually pleasing sensory items for the child to use when needed.

5. If a child shows interest in a work or material that he has not been introduced to yet, because of the visual component, do not hesitate to teach the child how to use the material correctly. Visual stimming can lead to extraordinary learning experiences.

Writing

A child with special needs may struggle with writing. Writing requires the development of the pincer grasp, a hand preference, and sufficient hand and muscle strength. It requires coordination and focus.

If a child has developmental disabilities or has demonstrated differences in the development of the brain, the emergence of writing skills may be delayed. A child with intellectual disabilities may struggle with the development of this skill. Those with physical disabilities may also have difficulties.

There are two aspects of writing that a child may have difficulties with. The first is the formation of letters and numbers. Second is the process of expressing one's thoughts accurately through writing.

Struggles with writing can often bring a child with special needs to tears. It can lead to some pretty significant behaviors as well. Writing tends to be the basic skill required to progress with learning, however in so many cases this does not need to be the case. There are many ways to learn that do not require a pen and paper.

Writing in a Montessori Classroom

Like all Montessori processes, learning to write does not begin with the language curriculum. It starts with Practical Life work that prepare little hands, strengthening muscles and develops the pincer grasp. To start the writing process before these are developed will only cause frustration and setbacks.

Once a child becomes successful with pre-writing focused Practical Life work tasks and has begun the process of learning letter sounds, it is appropriate to introduce writing. There are only two original Montessori writing materials in the early language curriculum. The first is called the Metal Insets. There are so many skills learned as a child traces shapes using the Metal Insets.

The Montessori Lower Case Cursive Sandpaper Letters is the other original Montessori writing material. For those who prefer to use the Montessori Lower Case Sandpaper Letters in print, they are available as well.

The Montessori Sandpaper Letters are used to teach children the shape of each letter. If one is teaching a child how to write numbers, the Montessori Sandpaper Numbers are used. No matter what Sandpaper Numbers or Letters are taught, the process of going through this work is crucial to helping the child learn how to write.

Sandpaper Letters are actually made of sandpaper. The cards provide a rich sensory experience for the child. The control of error is the texture. Once a child is successful with the Sandpaper Letters the Montessori Sand Tray is introduced. This is not an original Montessori material but is used in most Montessori schools.

Lowercase letters are taught first, a couple at a time. Letters do not need to be introduced in any specific order, just remember that they should not look or sound alike. When the child can successfully write letters in the sand tray, a chalkboard is introduced for practice in most Montessori schools.

When the child is successful at writing on the chalkboard with no lines, a chalkboard with lines is most often introduced. Once writing tasks come easy using a lined chalkboard, plain white paper and pencils are available for writing tasks in some Montessori schools. If a teacher feels no need to work with unlined paper, this step may be skipped.

Writing using lined paper and pencil is introduced last. The process of writing takes time and can not be rushed. Learning to write occurs at the same time a child is learning his numbers and letter sounds, once a teacher confirms the child is ready and has the proper skills to move forward.

The process of learning to write is child–led. If a child is not ready or interested, there is no push to learn the skill. Maria Montessori designed her materials in such a way that writing was not a prerequisite for learning. A child can advance in other subject areas without needing to write first.

The process of writing in a Montessori classroom is ideal for a child with special needs. Each and every step of the process benefits the child. As the teacher follows the child, he will be successful.

A Tip for Montessori Teachers

1. A child with special needs may find it easier to learn cursive letters first. It may be easier to identify the letters in cursive and write them with fewer errors and reversals. Another child may simply finds cursive letters easier to write, since they are made in one fluid movement.

Extra Tidbits

Independence

A child with special needs often lacks independence at home and in educational environments. The child relies on the help of parents or teachers to accomplish tasks related to life skills and school assignments. Home and educational environments are designed for adults in most cases, not allowing a child to reach his fullest potential. There is often a no-touch or do policy for the child in many situations throughout the day. The child learns to wait for the parent or teacher to complete tasks that he can complete himself. He becomes used to this process and it continues indefinitely.

This situation is quite ironic in that most parents of a child with special needs desperately want him to become as independent as possible. Their hope is that he can be successful at living independently as an adult in the future and be happy.

The goal of living independently and happily requires constant focus on academics and life skills in and outside the classroom Unfortunately, most academic settings are no longer teaching life skills and therefore are not preparing a child, especially one with special needs, for life in the real world. Parents often find themselves needing to work outside of the home to support their family, eliminating quality time that could be spent teaching life skills. Independence is impossible to achieve in these circumstances.

Independence in a Montessori Environment

Independence is not only encouraged in a Montessori environment, but the basis of learning. All furniture and materials used for work are child sized. A Montessori teacher is trained to not intervene or interrupt tasks that a child is able to successfully complete on his own, even if he struggles a bit. These same principles are encouraged in a Montessori home as well.

The teacher will offer assistance when the child asks. But even in these cases the teacher will not complete the task for the child. Instead she will provide guidance and direction so that the child can complete the task on his own if possible. Maria Montessori believed that the completion of a task without the assistance from an adult provides the self-satisfaction and drive the child needs to continue learning new things. The desire to move forward with learning does not come from the praise of others.

The Montessori curriculum does not just focus on reading, writing and arithmetic. It includes lessons necessary for success in all areas of life, including Grace and Courtesy lessons, Peace Education, Practical Life Skills, and Sensorial experiences. If a child continues with the Montessori Method during the middle school years, he is required to complete service hours within the community as part of the curriculum. In high school he is required to have a job. Montessori focuses on the development of the whole child, encouraging independence and self-sufficiency in all areas of life.

Tips for a Montessori Teacher

1. A child with special needs may have delays in fine and gross motor skills or developmental delays in multiple areas. Consider the developmental age of the child when choosing appropriate work and materials for him to use to ensure success and independence in all areas of learning.

2. At times a child with special needs may require adaptive equipment in the classroom to move around freely and/or complete tasks. Make sure this adaptive equipment is available to promote as much independence as possible.

Therapy

A child with special needs often participates in various types of therapy. Some of these include but are not limited to:

- Occupational Therapy
- Speech Therapy
- Physical Therapy

Occupational therapy is recommended to assist a child with special needs who struggles with daily life activities such as self-care, education, work, and social interactions. Therapy consists of activities that are aimed at helping the child in these areas, depending on his age. In many educational settings after preschool, occupational therapy focuses primarily on writing and skills that will help a child in school.

Speech therapy is recommended to assist a child with speech and language problems. Therapy consists of activities that are aimed at helping the child communicate clearly and accurately in conversation.

Physical therapy is recommended to assist a child with physical challenges caused by disease, injury, or disability. Therapy can include a variety of treatments which include: massage, exercise, water, electricity, heat and/or light.

Most often, before a child is school age, therapies take place in the home. Once a child attends school, therapy takes place in the classroom, or the child is pulled into another room to work with a therapist one-to-one. Therapy sessions vary in length but most often are 30 minutes to an hour long. The frequency of therapy in an educational setting is determined by a special education committee and can vary from one to five times a week.

If a child does not qualify for therapies in a school setting, parents can seek therapies elsewhere paying out of pocket. In some cases therapies may be covered by insurance. As one might guess, therapies can be very expensive. Time spent in therapies is minimal and can only have so much influence on the child.

Therapies in a Montessori Environment

Maria Montessori's first experiences educating children occurred in an asylum and the inner city slums. These children were considered unteachable and displayed multiple delays and disabilities. Her curriculum, materials, and method were first developed as she worked with these children. She knew they needed daily practice with tasks related to daily life skills as well as sensory stimulation to awaken or calm the body's senses.

The Practical Life and Sensorial curriculums meet these needs. These two curriculums combined with materials and work created to help a child write and read are occupational therapy at it's best. A child has access to these materials in the classroom on a daily basis and can select them from the shelves as often as he would like. As a child masters one skill, he moves on to the next, progressing at his own pace.

Maria Montessori recognized that children with special needs often need help in the areas of speech and language. Language work often includes hand-held materials for the child to manipulate and pictures as controls. The three period lesson is designed to help a child who struggles with speech issues as mentioned earlier. Lastly, Grace and Courtesy lessons are speech therapy. Lessons are incredibly helpful for a child who struggles with the etiquette associated with social situations.

If you are interested in learning more about Grace and Courtesy lessons and how they relate to speech therapy for children, especially those with ASD, I highly recommend Deb Chitwood's book, *Montessori at Home or School: How to Teach Grace and Courtesy.* It is amazing and includes all of the guidance you need.

Maria Montessori understood the need for movement in the classroom as well. She encouraged this through the design of the Montessori environment as well as work and materials on the shelves. A child in a Montessori environment is also encouraged to spend as much time outdoors as possible, which promotes physical activity. All of these ideas, most often the opposite of what's encouraged in public education today, provide sufficient opportunity and time for healthy physical development.

The Montessori Method truly encompasses everything a child may need to succeed in his educational pursuits and life skill functioning. It is through this method that a child can reach his highest potential and meet if not exceed the functioning and performance level of typical peers.

Tips for Montessori Teachers

1. Don't hesitate to create supplemental Practical Life and Sensorial works to help a child with special needs develop skills necessary for independence.
2. A child with ASD may need visuals and manipulatives when learning Grace and Courtesy lessons in order to fully understand them.
3. If a teacher has a child in the classroom with physical delays, be sure to select appropriate materials and works that encourage independence and success in this area.

4. A parent may not be aware that therapies are incorporated into the Montessori curriculum and request therapeutic intervention during class time. Take time to explain and introduce the parent to materials and work in the classroom and how they relate to the child's success and development.

Yes!

At times parents of a child with special needs feel discouraged. It is so easy to compare the child with typical peers, especially when all are expected to conform to the same standards of learning at specific chronological ages and are divided into classrooms by age to reinforce this concept.

It is easy for a child with special needs to feel discouraged when he is expected to perform at the same level as peers. This loss of confidence is made worse as a child in most educational settings is required to take tests and receive grades that supposedly reflect the child's knowledge on a given subject, when often times they don't accurately reflect the child's understanding of the subject.

Every child is different and develops at his own pace. This is particularly true with a child who has special needs. The cognitive, developmental, and emotional ages of the child may be different. Shouldn't he be able to learn at his own pace in an environment that encourages independence and self-sufficiency without a focus on how he compares to his peers? Shouldn't he be given ample time and space to succeed?

Maria Montessori says yes! She has created an amazing method for teaching that has proven successful with children who have special needs. The Montessori Method is child-focused and child-led. It contains all elements necessary for a child to achieve academic success and have the skills necessary to function independently in the real word if possible.

Every child can feel confident in his abilities because he demonstrates his capacity to learn each and every day at a pace that is comfortable, all the while pursuing his interests. Lessons are individualized and include materials that are applicable to every learning preference. Controls of error are provided so he can accomplish work on his own.

Does Montessori work for every child with special needs? Yes! As long as the teacher understands the child's behaviors, is willing to follow the child, and puts the proper supports in place, any child can thrive in a Montessori environment.

Zero Exceptions

This entire book has been dedicated to helping parents and Montessori teachers alike understand that Montessori really is for everyone including those with special needs. A child with special needs won't just function in a Montessori environment, he will thrive. But some may still be wondering if it can really work for EVERY child. Once again, I'm here to say yes! There are zero exceptions.

To illustrate this point, I'd like to end this book in a more personal way, talking about my youngest child, Sunshine who is now five years old. As mentioned in our family story, Sunshine was placed in our home as a foster child at the age of six months. She was taken from her parents at birth but experienced many hardships in a foster home previous to ours. Sunshine also faces many genetic challenges inherited from her birth parents. To date, Sunshine has received the following diagnoses:

- Mild Cranial Facial Microsomia
- Vision Impairment (related to Cranial Facial Microsomia)
- Food Allergies
- Developmental Delay
- Reactive Attachment Disorder (RAD)
- PTSD
- Autism Spectrum Disorder
- Mood Disorder

Sunshine is not an easy child. There are daily rages and bursts of physical aggression. Destructive tendencies are high. Anything can become a weapon. Behaviors related to RAD are constant. PTSD episodes occur frequently. Sunshine struggles with sensory issues, being extremely sensitive to auditory, tactile, and vestibular input and craving proprioceptive input. She has very little frustration tolerance. This child cannot sit still for more than ten seconds and is constantly on the move. Sunshine cannot slow down and requires on average two hours of rigorous physical activity a day just to stay regulated. On top of all this, she does not sleep through the night.

Chronologically, Sunshine is five years old, but developmentally she is two or three years old. Emotionally she is only two or three years old. Her cognitive age varies depending on if she is in a manic episode or not. During the time when Maria Montessori was alive, for all intents and purposes, Sunshine would have been labeled unteachable by society. In today's day and age, Sunshine still can't function in a public educational setting.

But here's the thing, she loves to learn. Her favorite part of the day is learning time. And despite all that's going on with her body and mind, she is learning. I owe this entirely to the Montessori Method. You see, we've tried other methods of learning. Nothing worked. Sunshine actually regressed. But when using the Montessori Method she continues to surprise us. Not only is she learning, but she's thriving.

Montessori isn't just an option for her, it's the only way Sunshine can succeed. And so it is with children who have similar special needs. There are zero exceptions. Even when Sunshine is at her worst, Montessori still works.

She may not be able to function in a Montessori classroom at this time because her mood disorder has not been stabilized, but she can function in a Montessori homeschooling environment with the proper support. The Montessori Method itself always works. There are zero exceptions.

It's my hope that this book will bridge the gaps between the special needs and Montessori world so that parents and teachers can better understand how to meet the needs of a child with special needs. The thing is, Maria Montessori included everything one might need with zero exceptions. It's all there, you just have to put it into practice!

About the Author

Renae M Eddy

Renae is a Montessori homeschooling mother of four special needs children with developmental and emotional disabilities. She blogs about her family's journey on the website Every Star Is Different, providing Montessori-inspired unit studies, syllabuses, activities, free printables and support for families with special needs. Before children, Renae was a musician. She holds a bachelor's degree in music with an emphasis in voice.